SO-AYF-088

Tell Me How It Reads

DATE DUE

PE
1404
.B2237
2012

Tell Me How It Reads

TUTORING DEAF AND HEARING STUDENTS IN THE WRITING CENTER

Rebecca Day Babcock

Gallaudet University Press
Washington, DC

KVCC KALAMAZOO VALLEY
COMMUNITY COLLEGE
LIBRARY

Gallaudet University Press

Washington, DC 20002
http://gupress.gallaudet.edu

© 2012 by Gallaudet University

All rights reserved. Published 2012

Printed in the United States of America

Library of Congress Cataloging-in-Publication Data

Babcock, Rebecca Day, 1968- author.
  Tell me how it reads : tutoring deaf and hearing students in the writing
center / Rebecca Day Babcock.
      pages cm
  Includes bibliographical references and index.
  ISBN 978-1-56368-547-7 (ebook) (print) — ISBN 978-1-56368-548-4
(pbk. : alk. paper)
  1. English language—Rhetoric—Study and teaching (Higher)
2. English language—Remedial teaching.   3. Deaf—Education (Higher)
4. Tutors and tutoring.   5. Writing centers.   I. Title.

  PE1404.B2237 2012
  808'.0420711--dc23   2012040195

ISBN 978-1-56368-548-4, 1-56368-548-5
E-book: ISBN 978-1-56368-547-7, 1-56368-547-7

∞ The paper used in this publication meets the minimum requirements of
American National Standard for Information Sciences—Permanence of
Paper for Printed Library Materials, ANSI Z39.48-1984.

Contents

Preface

For some time now, I have been interested in how writing centers can help all students. I am always looking for issues that provoke interest, cause writing center people to reflect on tutorial practices, and lead to improvement. Tutoring deaf students is one such issue. Compositionists and writing center professionals are interested in learning more about this topic, as evidenced in posts and questions raised regularly on WCenter (a listserv for writing center professionals) and the attendance at sessions on deafness and writing at the Conference on College Composition and Communication. Muriel Harris (pers. comm.), editor of the *Writing Lab Newsletter,* reports that people frequently inquire about articles on tutoring deaf students. The goal of my research is to raise awareness about providing quality tutoring services to all students who come into the writing center, beginning with this study of deafness and how it interacts with common tutoring practices. Ideally, the research as presented in this book will provide a model or at least describe practices for working with deaf students. Because of the need for published research studies on writing centers in general and tutoring deaf college students in particular, I am pleased to share my research with a wider audience through this book. I hope that what I have learned will improve tutoring for collge-level deaf students and that readers will be inspired to conduct their own studies.

The overarching question that informs the entire study is, what happens in a tutoring session between a deaf tutee and a hearing tutor? This question has three subparts:

1. What is the content of the tutorial (what material is covered) between a deaf tutee and a hearing tutor, and is it different from a tutorial between a hearing tutor and a hearing student?
2. How does the tutoring happen? What are the participants' roles and behaviors? What techniques are used?
3. What are the contributing and complicating factors: communication, affect, others?

The research goals and questions for this study evolved as I conducted it. In many qualitative studies, the research goals and questions evolve as the researcher learns more about the phenomenon at hand (Strauss and Corbin 1998). In this case, the goals remained stable while the research questions evolved. Even though the original questions are still valid, I learned while carrying out the research how to improve the arrangement and organization of the questions.

Theoretical and Experiential Framework

I offer this brief explanation of my personal beliefs and background to "come clean" as a biased, human, and fallible researcher.

Positionality Statement

I am a Caucasian, middle-class, hearing woman born in the 1960s. I have recently come to realize that I belong to a generation that is different from that of my own students and some of the participants in this study. I was raised in eastern Massachusetts and attended mostly public schools, up to and including university. I do not have any deaf people in my family, and my experience with and exposure to deaf people was limited before I engaged in this study. I have always been interested in linguistics, and it is that angle that most interests me in the study. I am also concerned with equality, social justice, and people's rights. I believe strongly that all people have the same rights even if they are different physically or mentally or in the way they approach life tasks. Many people who work with deaf people may be exploiting them or paternalizing them for their own gain (Lane 1992). I have examined myself and have not found any of the motives or feelings that Lane describes. I am grateful, however, that the participants have made it possible for me to complete this study. They have agreed to let me document them not just for me but for others who might be helped by this research. Foucault said, "[T]he turning of real lives into writing is no longer a procedure of heroization; it functions as a procedure of objectification and subjection" (quoted in Lane 1992, 81). I have done my best not to let this happen. By "member checking" (participant feedback), the participants let me know if they were not happy with the way they were portrayed, and I either changed the description or added their opinions as a form of polyvocality, so opinions and interpretations other than the author's could be represented.

Personal Beliefs and Research Assumptions

> Researchers will need to confront their own agendas and interpretive stances. . . . Researchers will need to articulate the assumptions that guide their research questions and acknowledge that research, by definition, is necessarily interested, limited, and partial, no matter what the methodology used. (Kirsch 1992, 258)

The following brief discussion, which is a response to Kirsch, is my attempt to meet the challenge of exploring and understanding my own assumptions and beliefs.

Personal Beliefs

I come to this study with various assumptions, prejudices, and personal opinions. I believe that writing centers should be open and available to all students. In the course of my research I called many writing centers to ask whether they ever tutored deaf students. I was frankly surprised at the number that said they did not tutor any students who had disabilities. The practice in some places is to send students who are different somewhere else to be tutored. In my opinion, this practice is wrong, and the basis of my research is to help writing center people feel more comfortable tutoring people who are different and to work on opening their doors to everybody. The fact that people who learn differently or are physically different are turned away from some writing centers is to me a very unfortunate situation.

Another one of my beliefs is inclusion, at least at the college level. I agree with Deaf educators and parents that mainstreaming for young deaf children in many cases is a recipe for isolation and failure. (The experience of Tonya Stremlau Johnson [1996] is an exception.) On the other hand, college students have the right to choose. Those who desire an all-deaf experience can choose to attend Gallaudet University or the National Technical Institute for the Deaf. In any case, all students should be able to get help in their school's writing center. If deaf students choose a mainstream school, they should be able to get the same help that other students do. That the writing center would turn away students who are different is inappropriate at best and discriminatory at worst. However, I do believe that students with disabilities may need extra tutoring or specialty tutoring in a disabilities services center, but that does not mean that the writing center should turn anyone away. The writing center community needs to make an effort to include all students in the services it offers.

Research Assumptions

First of all, I believe that writing centers are established and valid sites for the teaching and learning of writing. Previously, writing center scholars had to defend their existence and either complain about or revel in their marginality. But I maintain that writing centers have arrived. They no longer need to be defended. Second, since I limited my research to mainstream schools, I take for granted that the students in my study chose to enter a mainstream college program rather than an all-deaf context, like that at Gallaudet. Of course, some students may have wanted to go to Gallaudet but were prevented by economic or other reasons.

My Theoretical Foundation

My theoretical foundation is mostly social constructivist. This position is in agreement with Lincoln and Guba (2000):

We believe that a goodly portion of social phenomena consists of the meaning-making activities of groups and individuals around those phenomena. The meaning-making activities themselves are of central interest to social constructivists/constructionists simply because it is the meaning-making/sense-making/attributional activities that shape action (or inaction). (167)

What makes this concept relevant to this study is that, in tutoring sessions, tutors and tutees are in a constant state of "meaning-making/sense-making" activities, even to the point of continually asking each other, "Does that make sense?" The following characteristics of constructivism guide the study: The "relationship to foundations of truth and knowledge" is antifoundational (173). The control is shared by the researcher and the participants. The nature of knowledge is "individual reconstructions coalescing around consensus" or, in this case, the possibility of polyvocality (Lincoln and Guba 2000, 170).

I classify myself and my research as postmodern, as there is no truth other than what my participants and I construct out of language, and even then each person in the exchange creates a different meaning and a different reality out of that discourse. The resulting document should be viewed as a postmodern pastiche of styles and voices.

Ethical Concerns

The "basic ethical principles that underlie all scholarly writing" serve "to ensure the accuracy of scientific and scholarly knowledge" and "to protect intellectual property rights" (American Psychological Association 2001, 348). In contrast, my greatest ethical concerns in this study were not to harm the participants in any way and to properly and fairly represent them. I wanted to make sure I found no bad news, so I carefully tried to find research sites that were doing good work with deaf students. But since people are human and the activity of tutoring is extremely complex, it was almost impossible to find *only* positive experiences and 100-percent effective tutoring practices. My main ethical issue was how to deal with this bad news.

Researchers can sometimes feel uncomfortable if they find "bad news" or are critical of "participants' actions, comments and attitudes" (Kirsch 1999, 55). I am acutely aware of these feelings. To properly represent participants' voices I have submitted to them all of the transcripts and drafts, and some have asked me to remove all instances of "umm" and "you know" from the interview transcripts. I gladly did that. Also, if there was anything that would reflect negatively on a participant in any way (e.g., a tutoring technique that did not work), I planned to use double anonymity. That means I would not even identify the person by the pseudonym used in the study. I would just use the title (e.g., tutor, tutee, interpreter, administrator). In this way I hoped I would not hurt anyone's feelings if I had to be critical of a certain event or practice because of what I found in the study.

In the resulting write-up I determined that by attempting to objectively portray tutoring as it happened, I was giving a fair portrayal of participants, and, as I wrote, I became more comfortable. I was concerned with not hurting anyone's feelings. By inviting me into their writing and tutoring centers, letting me observe their tutoring sessions, and talking to me, the participants were so open and accommodating that I could not betray that trust by showing them or their practices in a negative light. On the other hand, I owe it to my readers, grantmakers, and future tutees everywhere to discuss techniques that are not as effective so that people may learn from them. I thank my participants again for this opportunity and for exposing themselves to this potential vulnerability. I did my best to maintain their trust and represent them fairly. Whenever a participant and I disagreed, through the member-checking procedure that participant had an opportunity to write a comment or response to be included in the discussion. I realize that this practice of member checking is not entirely fair, as participants might not have the spare time to devote to lengthy feedback activities (Kirsch 1999).

I also shared what I was learning with my participants along the way. I gave presentations to tutors and answered questions from them both in person and by phone and email. I did not withhold any information from the participants. In addition, I shared the tentative conclusions I was drawing and discussed meaning-making possibilities with the participants. This practice is in accordance with the recommendations of

Strauss and Corbin (1998), who suggest that researchers should bring their emerging understandings back to the participants to check them for accuracy. Strauss and Corbin intend this technique to result in richer and more accurate data, but I see it more as an ethical issue. Kirsch (1999) maintains that this practice can result in research that is better both epistemologically and ethically—in the end, research that is "more detailed, rich, and nuanced" (11). I respect the knowledge of all of the participants—as we learned from each other we created the knowledge and meanings reported here. I felt strange when the participants treated me as an expert, and I deflected such statements with what I hoped was humor and humility.

Acknowledgments

I WOULD LIKE TO thank my family, especially Mike Babcock and Aileen, David, and Kristen Day, for supporting me in this research, the International Writing Centers Association and the Rock Valley College Foundation for funding the research, my professors Ben Rafoth, Rich Nowell, and Nancy Hayward for their feedback, and the research participants for the kind gift of their time and knowledge. I would especially like to thank the circulation and reference librarians at Indiana University of Pennsylvania, Kishwaukee College, Rock Valley College, Rockford Public Library, and Howard Colman Library. Thanks also to Ceil Lucas and colleagues for important linguistic analysis, to my writing group members Anthony Edgington and Randall McClure for their useful comments, and to Charlie Hicks and Julie McCown for their assistance.

Tell Me How It Reads

CHAPTER 1

———

Introduction

Shortly after I began directing the writing center at the University of Texas at Brownsville, two deaf students began coming in for tutoring. This event not only disrupted our routine but also sparked an ongoing interest in the complicated and multifaceted topic of tutoring deaf students at mainstream hearing postsecondary institutions. Common tutoring practices used with hearing students do not necessarily work for deaf people, and some of the tutors in this case actually shied away from and tried to avoid tutoring the deaf women. This exposure to deaf student writers clearly made the tutors uncomfortable. In *Good Intentions,* Nancy Grimm (1999) writes of a tutor whose discomfort with a student's unconventional literacy practices inspired her dissertation research. Unease or embarrassment in a classroom or tutoring session may also serve as a prompt to work toward a better understanding of different ways to help student writers (Kirsch 1992).

This unease and desire to know more resulted in a naturalistic study of writing tutorials with deaf college students in both writing and learning centers. I observed tutorials and conducted interviews with d/Deaf and hearing students, their tutors, their interpreters, and the directors of the writing and learning centers where they were tutored.[1] I conducted research at two different colleges: a four-year private college in a major Midwestern city that offers undergraduate and graduate majors in the visual, performing, media, and communications arts, which I call Davis College, and a suburban community college near this same Midwestern city, which I call Stanhope College. As I relate in more detail later, the choice of colleges was based on convenience factors such as proximity to my house, friendliness and helpfulness of staff and contact people, availability of deaf students being tutored, and willingness to participate.

This book is based on the resulting study of tutoring in writing in the college context with both deaf and hearing students and their tutors, describing in detail tutoring sessions between deaf students, hearing tutors, and the interpreters that help them communicate. Although a description of other methods of communication, such as written notes on paper (Schmitz 2008, 138) would be valuable, the deaf tutees I observed all chose to conduct their tutoring sessions through an interpreter. In addition, all of the tutees in this study chose to use a variety of English or contact signing rather than American Sign Language (ASL) in the tutorials.[2] The ultimate goal of describing these tutorials is to illustrate the key differences between deaf-hearing and hearing-hearing tutorials and to suggest ways to modify tutoring and tutor-training practices accordingly. Although this study describes the tutoring of deaf students, the focus on students who learn differently can inform the tutoring of students with learning disabilities, English as a second language (ESL) students, and other nonmainstream students or students with different learning styles. In addition, through the results of grounded theory analysis, this book offers a complete paradigm for all tutoring of writing.

Deaf students are attending mainstream postsecondary institutions in increasing numbers. Seventy-three percent of all US institutions of higher education reported enrolling students who were deaf or hard of hearing. These students account for 4 percent of all students with disabilities

---

1. Throughout the book I use "Deaf" with a capital "D" to indicate cultural deafness, "deaf" with a lowercase "d" to indicate auditory deafness, and "d/Deaf" to consciously include both groups. I use "deaf" generally throughout the document as a neutral term and use "d/Deaf" or "Deaf" where the distinction is relevant.
2. I thank Ceil Lucas of Gallaudet University for confirming the participants' language choices in the tutorial.

at these institutions (Raue and Lewis 2011). According to Watson et al. (2007) there are 414,300 college students in the United States with some form of hearing loss, but not all these students disclose their condition, nor do they all ask for accommodation. However, current literature says little about tutoring this mainstream deaf population, and even less has been written about conducting tutoring sessions using sign language interpreters. Writing tutorials conducted through communication modes based on English, such as lipreading and speaking, as well as writing—both on paper and computer screens—have been documented, but these were mostly first-person narrative accounts of tutoring a single deaf student. Other than my work (Babcock 2008, 2011), no documentation exists of mainstream college writing tutorials conducted through an interpreter, although Roy (2000) studied an interpreted teacher-student conference with a graduate student, his professor, and an interpreter. Like Roy's, this study is an outsider's view of the process, but rather than being a case study of a single conference with a single student, this study is designed to expand the view on this subject by focusing on multiple conferences with multiple students that rely on the use of interpreters. Through interviews with all of the participants, this study attempts to show the perspectives of everyone involved (i.e., researcher, tutee, tutor, interpreter, and administrator) and how these perspectives illustrate the content and techniques of the tutoring sessions, as well as the interpersonal factors involved.

Today, more deaf students are attending mainstream programs than in the past, and there is little written in the tutoring literature about this population. For academic communities interested in helping all students, especially those with disabilities, a study of this type is a first step in understanding the complex situation of tutoring deaf college students in writing. In addition, of all the research articles in the writing center literature about tutoring deaf students, no other researcher mentions the use of an interpreter, which, according to my study participants, is an extremely effective way to tutor deaf students. This study details the use of an interpreter in tutorials with deaf students and hearing tutors.

The study data set consisted of a total of thirty-six interviews and nineteen tutoring sessions with sixteen participants, along with a collection of related documents and general observations. The participants included all of the stakeholders involved in tutoring deaf students in writing at two institutions where a minimum of two tutoring sessions between a deaf student and a hearing tutor could be observed. Interviews and observations at three other institutions were conducted; however, there was no opportunity to meet the two-tutoring-session minimum, so these data were not included in the main analysis, but the study refers to these sessions and interviews anecdotally where appropriate.

At Davis College I observed tutoring sessions with two different deaf writers and three different hearing writers working with the same two tutors. At Stanhope College I observed two tutoring sessions with a deaf student and a hearing tutor and had an additional session taped for me. In addition to interviewing the tutors, tutees, and interpreters involved in these sessions, I interviewed the director and the assistant director of the writing center at Davis and the director of the Academic Success Center and the director of Disabilities Services at Stanhope. The numbers of interviews varied at each place because I conducted a minimum of one interview with each participant and scheduled further interviews based on the participant's availability and my need for more information (for full observation and interview data see table 1).

Tutoring Deaf Students

It is important to present the literature about tutoring in writing and the education of deaf students, especially the intersection of the two. Rather than covering all of the pertinent reading, I present here only the background information and more current scholarship immediately relevant to the ensuing discussion; in particular I do not cover older studies (e.g., Ameter and Dahl 1990) or literature that does not relate to the face-to-face tutoring of deaf college students. For instance, I do not include articles about elementary-level tutoring or computer-based tutoring. Other texts are discussed as needed throughout the chapters.

Current Writing Center Practice

Writing center practice has followed a narrative of progress from current traditional or positivist assumptions through expressivist tenets, to the

TABLE 1. *Observation and Interview Data*

Tutoring Sessions	
Deaf Tutees, Hearing Tutors, and Interpreters	**Number of Observations**
Rae, John, and Linda	3
Blue, Newby, and Linda	1
Blue, Newby, and Jay	4
Kali, Gustav, and Melissa	2
Hearing Tutees and Hearing Tutors	**Number of Observations**
Shareef and John	3
Herrodrick and John	3
Squirt and Newby	2
Interviews	
Deaf Tutees	**Number of Interviews**
Rae	3
Blue	4
Kali	2
Hearing Tutees	**Number of Interviews**
Shareef	2
Herrodrick	1
Squirt	1
Tutors	**Number of Interviews**
John	6
Newby	6
Gustav	2
Interpreters	**Number of Interviews**
Linda	2
Jay	2
Melissa	1
Administrators	**Number of Interviews**
Ann	1
Brock	1
Ted	1
Daisy	1

recent trend toward social constructivism. Lunsford (1991) calls these practices the "Storehouse," the "Garret," and the "Burkean Parlor." The storehouse refers to the distribution of accepted knowledge and the outcome of an improved paper. This is associated with a product-based approach and directive tutoring where the tutor has the answers and explicitly directs the writer on how to revise his or her paper. The garret center is based on a Romantic or an expressivist approach, in which all truth and creativity reside within the writer. In this approach the tutor's job is to use Socratic questioning to allow the knowledge that is within the writer to emerge. The focus is on process rather than product, and the writer's true voice and desire to communicate are valued rather than objective correctness. In the Burkean Parlor, collaboration reigns. The tutor and the tutee come together as equals to discuss a paper with the expectations of the discourse community never too far out of the picture.

Some common writing center practices are reading the paper aloud (either by the tutor or the tutee), the concepts that the student "owns" the paper and that the tutor should neither write on the paper nor offer words and language to the tutee, and the use of nondirective questioning techniques, sometimes known as "hands-off" or "minimalist" tutoring. A nondirective question might be "Why did you put a comma here?" rather than just telling the student the rule for using a comma. Several of these common practices become problematic when working with deaf tutees.

Tutor Training

Lennard Davis (1995) wrote that deafness—and disability in general—have been undertheorized. Fifteen percent of Americans have a disability, and 10 percent of the population has a hearing loss (881). Deafness is a unique situation in which many commonplace ideas about language become problematic, such as the way people may think of an author *speaking* through a text. Davis claims that this can cause writers who handle language differently to be left out of the metaphor. Commonly, writing and reading are referred to in analogies of hearing and speaking, and common tutoring practices depend on aural and oral processing of language. Deaf people, in contrast, process language primarily through the eyes and hands, not the ears and the mouth. For tutoring, an understanding of different modalities of language processing (e.g., visual) can help tutors assist students with learning disabilities and different learning styles. Tutor training sometimes focuses on helping students who learn differently, but a quick look at tutor guides reveals little emphasis on physical difference. According to my research, in the last twenty years only one general tutor training book (Arkin and Shollar 1982) has addressed more than a sentence or two to deafness until Murphy and Sherwood's (2003) *St. Martin's Sourcebook for Writing Tutors* included Margaret Weaver's (1996) article about tutoring a deaf student in a writing center. Including a component on deaf students in tutor training is important, as common peer-tutoring practices such as reading papers aloud are effective for auditory learners, but as Weaver (1996) writes, they appear to exclude the deaf student and others who process language differently. Through this study of tutoring deaf students, which focuses on sites accessible to deaf students, writing center practitioners, classroom teachers, and compositionists can not only learn from the experience and expertise of those involved but also begin to include deafness as an important linguistic and cultural category for theorizing, teaching, and tutor training.

Perspective

Most of the articles in the writing center literature have been first-person accounts of tutoring a deaf student. Faerm (1992) wrote of her experience tutoring Anne, a student who, although deaf from birth, did not sign but rather voiced and read lips. Anne had trouble understanding poetry. Because of her deafness, she could not perceive rhythm, stress, and, of course, the sound of language, which is so important in poetry. Marron (1993) responded to Faerm with her experience of tutoring a deaf student, and Wood (1995) and Weaver (1996) also reported their experiences working one-on-one with deaf students. All of these articles provided a single perspective—that of the tutor, although Weaver did include interviews with Anissa, the deaf student whom she tutored. Nash (2008) also gives a first-person account from experience, and Schmitz (2008), who interviewed deaf college students about their literacy learning experiences, acknowledges that her study would have been enhanced had she interviewed teachers as well.

Communication

Lang (2002) mentions the need for research on the use of interpreters in higher education. Few articles in the writing center literature discuss the use of interpreters for communication. Articles in the deaf studies and deaf education literature display the same limitation (e.g., Lang et al. 2004). For tutoring sessions, Faerm (1992), Marron (1993), and Weaver (1996) all relate the use of lipreading, while Wood (1995) describes the use of a computer for communication. Nash (2008), Schmidt et al. (2009), and Davis and Smith (2000) briefly discuss the use of interpreters but do not present the results of an actual study.

Lang et al. (2004) find that deaf college students prefer tutors who can communicate fluently with a variety of communication styles, but the tutoring sessions in their study took place at a special college program for deaf students, and the tutorials took place without interpreters. Davis and Smith (2000) discuss various communication methods that can be used to tutor deaf students, including speechreading, writing notes, and the use of an interpreter. Gail Wood (1995) explains a specific communication practice for working with deaf students, but readers need to be cautious about the title ("Making the Transition from ASL to English: Deaf Students, Computers, and the Writing Center") as not all deaf students use ASL. Wood describes her work with Jack, a deaf man fluent in ASL who had attended Gallaudet University. Wood decided not to work with an interpreter but instead to conduct the entire tutorial in writing, using a computer's word-processing software. Wood's emphasis on the use of the L2 (English) during the conference mirrors the practice of many writing centers that tutor ESL students in English only, for practice in the target language. Conducting the tutorial exclusively in English is a good idea intuitively, but then again, perhaps the use of interpreters would lessen the writers' communication anxiety. Marron (1993) and her deaf tutee, Susan, conversed through written notes, and Marron read Susan's paper aloud. After a while Marron "became comfortable and felt silly reading her text aloud, which I obviously was doing for my sake, not hers" (15). This is a key point: When one works with deaf students, reading the text aloud appears to be more for the benefit of the tutor than the student.

Tutoring Methods

In an ERIC report on tutoring deaf students, Orlando, Gramley, and Hoke (1997) mention a lack of research on tutoring deaf and hard of hearing students. Since then, the only actual studies of tutoring a deaf student in a mainstream context with an interpreter have been mine (Babcock 2008, 2009, 2011). Although the ERIC report lists tips and ideas for tutoring deaf students, the writers' portrayal of this tutoring is at variance with that generally accepted by composition and writing center scholars. The approach presented in the ERIC report is fairly directive and rigid, in contrast to the collaborative approach favored in writing center literature. Actually, the tutoring model in this ERIC report conforms closely to Lunsford's (1991) notion of a "storehouse," where knowledge is stored and handed out as needed. A more flexible approach such as Lunsford's "Burkean Parlor," where knowledge is socially constructed, allows for options for differences in writing processes and tutor/student preferences and learning styles.

Also problematic is the notion that tutors will identify "indications that the student has not correctly understood/applied certain relevant concepts" (Orlando, Gramley, and Hoke 1997, 8) and then correct them. This is outside the realm of a writing center tutorial, where the tutee is supposed to be the expert on content (Greiner 2000; Hubbuch 1988; McAndrew and Reigstad 2001). The other recommendations pertain to tutoring grammar, editing, and suggesting that the student "take [the paper] to the writing lab for corrections." Gillespie and Lerner (2000) discuss the difference between an editor and a tutor and insist that writing center tutors should resist the temptation to edit student papers. However, it may be that deaf writers do need an editor and that deaf and hard of hearing students need more grammatical direction than hearing students.

Moreover, the tutors in the writing lab need training, too. The report writers do not mention how tutors are to correct these errors. Are they to write on the student's paper? Explain the corrections through an interpreter? Most likely they cannot resort to reading the paper aloud and have the student listen for errors. The report writers have pushed writing lab tutors into the role of correctors of errors without mentioning the writing process at all or referring to any standard source material from the writing center field. Davis and Smith (2000) mention the importance of grammar when working with deaf students, and they also remind tutors not to simply proofread the paper for the student. In addition, they suggest tips for discussing organization and style.

Language

Deaf people in the United States use a variety of language and communication modes, styles, and varieties. A deaf person may communicate through written or spoken English or one or more varieties of signed language ranging from signed codes representing English, to American Sign Language, to contact sign, which can display features of both English and ASL. In stark contrast to the reality, stereotypes abound surrounding deaf people and their language. The range of stereotypes is broad and can include beliefs that all deaf people can speak English and read lips or that all deaf people in the United States know and can use American Sign Language (ASL). The reality falls somewhere in between (Nash 2008). Even professionals who work with deaf people—and deaf people themselves—are susceptible to these erroneous judgments. Some (e.g., Schmidt et al. 2009; Davis and Smith 2000) assume that deaf people's use of ASL *causes* errors in English, a point of view that I call the "contrastive analysis fallacy." I discuss (and reject) this fallacy elsewhere (Babcock 2006). Many people, including linguists, hold folk beliefs about language, and it is important not to fall into that trap. For instance, Marron (1993), Wood (1995), and Weaver (1996) all write that their deaf tutees used American Sign Language. But they do not indicate their own fluency in ASL or their criteria for judgment. Merely using a form of sign language or even reporting the use of ASL does not necessarily make it true. I myself know only a bit of English signing, and while conducting this research I had no reason to doubt the two participants who said they used ASL. However, when I sent a DVD of their signing to Ceil Lucas, a linguist at Gallaudet, I learned that they were actually using contact sign, which makes use of a combination of ASL and English. Marron (1993) also related that she learned a bit of sign language to put her tutee at ease. The fact that Marron claims that her tutee used ASL is also suspect. Unless Marron or her tutee had training in ASL linguistics, they would not be able to make this determination.

Culture

Since Deaf people are a cultural minority, it is important to study how aspects of Deaf culture interact with the tutoring process, but also to remember that not all deaf people are members of the Deaf culture. In fact, out of 36 million people in the United States with some form of hearing loss, approximately 500,000 are culturally Deaf, meaing they use ASL and "share behavioral norms, values, customs, educational institutions, and organizations" (Fileccia 2011). With regard to tutoring techniques, Deaf culture's value of directness may be in direct contrast to many writing centers' value of nondirective tutoring. Other cultural factors may or may not influence tutoring sessions, as the following chapters demonstrate.

Intercultural communication is a salient factor in tutoring writing (Eckard and Staben 2000; Gillespie and Lerner 2000; Harris 1986; Hayward 2004; McAndrew and Reigstad 2001). However, since most tutor-training books offer minimal information on Deaf culture, I refer to *Reading between the Signs* (Mindess 1999), a book on intercultural communication for sign language interpreters, as some of Mindess's points prove relevant to tutoring. I also refer to other books on Deaf culture where appropriate.

Deaf people value direct communication, or "straight talk," because communication and information are important commodities in the Deaf community (Mindess 1999). Deaf people do not have the privilege of overhearing incidental information in daily life:

> Hinting and vague talk in an effort to be polite are inappropriate and even offensive in the DEAF-WORLD. . . . A principle of etiquette in the DEAF-WORLD seems to be "always act in a way that facilitates communication." Hence, blunt speech is not rude, but sudden departures, private conversations, and breaking visual contact are. (Lane, Hoffmeister, and Bahan 1996, 73–74)

Nondirective tutoring techniques, for example, sometimes prove extremely frustrating for Deaf students who know the tutor has the information that they need and seemingly withholds it. Even more than simply frustrating, using nondirective techniques with Deaf students may be culturally insensitive, inappropriate, or even rude.

Another cultural factor is time. Many programs limit tutoring sessions to thirty minutes, and to accommodate back-to-back scheduling, sessions must begin and end promptly. Such a rigid scheduling system could be a problem for deaf students for a variety of reasons. For instance, Deaf people value context. When asked what a hearing person would consider a "simple yes-or-no question," they may start at the very beginning and narrate all of the factors leading up to the answer (Mindess 1999). Not only might this be frustrating for tutors who are unaware of Deaf culture, but with the addition of factors such as time needed for written notes or interpretation, sessions with Deaf students also have the potential to run long.

This in turn could cause another cultural miscommunication related to leave taking. Deaf people value long, extended leave takings and may feel that relating to the person they are with is more important than hurrying off to another appointment. I did not notice factors like time and leave taking as relevant to this particular study, probably because all of the sessions I observed were weekly, standing appointments. The one session in which time was a factor was seventy-five minutes long and was conducted entirely by writing on paper. It was not included in the final data set. Nevertheless, it is important for tutors to have an awareness of Deaf culture, as these issues could very well arise in tutorials in other contexts. Another aspect to consider is that deaf people have a lot of experience interacting with hearing people, although hearing people may have no experience at all interacting with deaf people. The interpreter can also serve as a cultural informant for both parties in the exchange. Mindess's (1999) book stresses the role of the interpreter as cultural liaison.

Books and articles on Deaf culture (Hall 1989; Mindess 1999) stress deaf people's tendency to hug and touch more than hearing people do. Deaf people use touch to get another person's attention. Other ways to get a deaf person's attention is to wave in the range of the person's peripheral vision or to make vibrations by tapping on an object, such as a table. I had anticipated that this tendency of Deaf people to engage in more physical touch might be a source of discomfort for tutors, but again, deaf people as a whole have more experience with hearing people and their ways than hearing people do with deaf people. There were no issues raised in the study related to hugging or touching. Nevertheless, tutors should be aware of this difference between Deaf and hearing cultures.

Tutors working with deaf students should also be aware of certain conventions and necessities when conversing with a deaf person, with or without an interpreter. Since deaf people cannot hear all sounds, if the interlocutor is called away or distracted by a noise, the deaf person might not know what is going on. The polite thing to do is to explain the interruption to the deaf person (Hall 1989). Also, in Deaf culture it is considered rude to leave without an explanation of one's absence. In hearing culture it is acceptable to say, "Excuse me for a moment," without an explanation of where one is going. It might even be considered too much information for hearing interlocutors to voluntarily add their destination, especially if it relates to body functions like using the toilet or blowing one's nose. Deaf people, on the other hand, expect a detailed explanation even for a brief absence (Mindess 1999).

These are just a few examples of the aspects of Deaf culture that have been observed and written about that may pertain to tutoring. Of course, there may be additional relevant factors, both cultural and individual, that have not been recorded. The important thing is for tutors to remain open and flexible when working with students of different cultural backgrounds. Most important, tutors can approach interpreters, whose role is not only to interpret words but also to interpret and educate interlocutors about Deaf cultural factors and expectations.

This discussion points out that, for writing center practitioners, disability in general and deafness in particular are issues of interest and concern, although they are underrepresented in tutor-training materials. The current descriptive study of tutoring writing in a postsecondary context with both deaf and hearing students presents a baseline that I hope will fill in some of the gaps. In addition, it further inquires into and expands on the ideas presented here by describing the content of and the techniques used in tutoring sessions involving a deaf tutee and a hearing tutor.

It can also inform our work with a larger group of students who learn differently. For instance, although the needs of deaf students are unique, their writing and learning styles and abilities present very interesting parallels to those of ESL students and students with learning disabilities.

The study also recognizes other important factors such as cultural matters that influence tutoring sessions with deaf students (see Weaver 1996). Deaf people as a cultural minority present challenges to tutors and administrators to be sensitive to their cultural differences. Another important aspect of the study is the investigation of the use of an interpreter during writing conferences that involve a hearing tutor and a deaf student. Through my research I have found that the use of an interpreter in such exchanges is fairly common, but no other research study in the writing center literature mentions it. This study along with Babcock (2011) is the first one to investigate the use of an interpreter in tutorials with deaf students and hearing tutors.

———

Deaf Tutees

THE STORIES OF the various participants in this study are interspersed throughout the chapters. First I present the profiles of the deaf tutees. The rest will follow in the remaining chapters. For this study I took a cultural rather than a clinical view of deafness. For instance, I did not gather information about students' levels of hearing loss and residual hearing, as these are audist concepts that regard hearing as the norm and deafness as a deviation from that norm. This is a medical model of deafness. Instead, I took the cultural view that deaf people are neither deviant nor deficient and that it is unnecessary for them to become more like hearing people. Rather, they constitute a cultural and linguistic minority whose only disability is that our society is geared toward hearing people. However, one cannot simply assume that every deaf person uses ASL or is a member of the Deaf community. There are many ways to be deaf, and not all deaf people are culturally Deaf.

Rae

Rae[3] was a tutee at Davis College at the time of the study. She is a twenty-five-year-old deaf white woman. Since her participation in the study,

———

3. The participants either chose their own pseudonyms or asked me to choose one for them. The more interesting and unique ones are those they chose.

Rae has left college, changed her career plans, and decided to become a stuntwoman or a wild animal trainer. Rae is a small woman who shops at the Whole Foods supermarket, reads *Organic Style,* and considers herself an environmentalist. She appeared to be popular among the college students and staff; the assistant director, Brock, recommended her as my first observation, I believe, because of her easygoing yet plucky personality.

Rae characterizes her language use as Pidgin Signed English (PSE). She explained to me that she had first learned to sign in English word order and was later exposed to ASL at the state[4] school for the deaf (SSD), which she attended from 1992 to 1996. Her signing now incorporates elements of ASL and English, which is called *contact signing* (and is also referred to as PSE). Attendance at a residential school is an important factor in Deaf acculturation (Lane, Hoffmeister, and Bahan 1996). Rae enrolled at Davis as a film student and first came to the writing center to get help with her learning disability.

In the 2003 spring semester, Rae had a standing, weekly two-hour appointment with John, her tutor. They began working on her film-class assignments, but after she dropped that class, most of their tutoring focused on her Spanish history class. Rae and John made a good match for the effectiveness of the tutorial. Rae knew what she needed and told John what she wanted to work on in the sessions. In the first tutorial I observed, she said the following to John:

> So, what I'd like you to do is just to check out my paper, just to, you know, edit it, make sure it makes sense. I'm not totally finished with it. I do have a lot more to go, but I'd like to get your feedback about what I should do next, what more information I should add to it.[5]

In a way, Rae was the ideal tutee as she took charge of the session and was able to articulate her goals.

---

4. I withhold the name of the state for confidentiality reasons.
5. All of the deaf people's words are as voiced by an interpreter. Therefore, the reader should pay attention to general sense and meaning rather than particulars of grammar and word choice. Some of the material has been edited for readability.

In the past, Rae had been tutored by an expert in ASL, and she appreciated that. She had also been tutored by an instructor at the college who asked inappropriate questions and wasted her time. Rae felt comfortable giving feedback to the assistant director of the writing center about what kind of tutor she did or did not want. One of her other preferences was directness: "I guess in Deaf culture people are rather direct as opposed to someone going on and on without getting to the point of what they're trying to say."

Rae knew what she wanted to work on, and she told the tutor about it. She was not the type of passive tutee that many tutors complain about. This part of her personality made her a model tutee. Also, John said she was interested, and he liked that. The Davis College Tutoring in Writing Skills Responsibilities Form states that the writer's role is to "bring in writing and/or have some idea about which aspect of writing you want to work on in each session." Rae clearly did this. She also met the other requirements of her role, which were to "ask questions, draw on the consultant's experience and knowledge, make suggestions, act on suggestions, and take a sincere interest in your writing and in improving your writing." She clearly wanted to work with her tutors, and she gave the following advice for tutors who would be working with deaf people: "Help them out. Show them what makes sense and what doesn't make sense. And if the deaf student asks why, then be patient with your answer. Answer the question and be clear. Most important is really to be patient with the deaf student because English is not often their first language."

Blue

At the time of the study, Blue was a nineteen-year-old acting major and a tutee in the writing center at Davis College. She is a young black woman who is interested in dancing; I confirmed this with her after reading a paper she wrote about a dance she created with her family for her grandmother's birthday party. I also noted the presentation she did about Janet Jackson, who interested her as a dancer. Blue is very motivated to learn and enjoys the time she spends with her tutor. In an interview she said this:

> Well, honestly, I feel pretty motivated to learn how to write. I feel like I'm ready to do it. You know, I feel more like I want to learn about verbs and adjectives. I feel pretty inspired to get that information and to learn about it.

In addition, she said she would like to improve her reading and English vocabulary. During the course of the study she was singled out as the most improved tutee, an honor that carried a cash award. She was nominated by her tutor, Newby, who also won a cash award for submitting her name.

Like Rae, Blue attended the SSD. She graduated from City Vocational Career Academy (CVCA).[6] At SSD she was exposed to ASL, but she reported that deaf students at CVCA signed differently. She reported that at SSD "there was more expressiveness, more joking capability, more social humor. But it seems there wasn't really much of that going on in the language [at CVCA]." She prefers that other people use ASL, but she is not really sure whether she prefers English or ASL in an academic context. Her interpreter, Jay, says that she tends to transliterate (interpret word for word from spoken to signed English) with Blue in the tutoring session.

The first semester I met Blue she was taking Intro to College Writing, and the second semester she was taking English Composition I. In the tutorial she also discussed work for her science class. She felt that her writing had improved greatly as a result of coming to the tutorials. The main issue she wanted to work on in the tutoring sessions was grammar, and through the tutoring sessions she was able to learn how to correct her own errors. She said the idea that grammar was important came from her teachers. She also wanted to work on understanding her homework assignments. Although she appreciated having an interpreter present during the tutoring sessions, she did not mind conducting the conferences in writing without an interpreter.

---

6. Name of the city withheld for confidentiality reasons.

When I asked Blue why she chose Davis instead of Gallaudet (the only liberal arts college exclusively for deaf students), she replied that she preferred to live at home rather than in a dorm. Also, at SSD she had not liked the food, and I think she generalized her opinion to include all residence halls. She currently lives with her mother, her mother's boyfriend, and her siblings. One of her brothers is also deaf, and her mother works for a shipping company. Blue said she would like to move into her own apartment. She was looking for a job the summer I met her but had not found one by the following fall, when our observations were complete.

Kali

Kali is a twenty-two-year-old Hispanic deaf woman. Her dad is deaf, and her mother, now deceased, was hard of hearing. She has one brother and two sisters, and one of whom is hard of hearing. Kali is originally from Texas, and her grandparents were from Mexico. Her paternal grandparents speak Spanish, her maternal grandmother spoke English, and her paternal grandfather spoke English and Spanish. In my research I learned that most deaf parents of deaf children use ASL at home with their children and that deaf and hearing children of deaf parents grow up using ASL as a first language. In Kali's case, her parents used a mix of ASL and English-like signing at home. Since Kali's mother and sister were hard of hearing, this makes sense, as many hard of hearing people use signs in English word order. Kali reported her parents would also use English-like signing with her hearing siblings. Avid readers, her parents ordered adult-level magazines such as *National Geographic, Time,* and *Life* for their children to read. As a deaf child of deaf parents, Kali is different from many deaf students in that she has a firm basis in language that allows her to read at an appropriate level (Mayer 2007). She prefers English-type signing, frequently fingerspells, and prefers interpreters who transliterate word for word so she can get the exact English that the tutor or teacher is using. As she told me in an interview,

> I have been a bookworm since I was little. So I really loved reading a lot. But writing was not my strength. Recently I became used

to—I'm learning my skill in writing. And so I'm trying to push
myself to write more, more than I have before.

In college, Kali is developing an interest in writing.

Kali attended various schools and often missed classes since her
dad moved around because of his work as a roofer. She attended both
deaf and mainstream programs at Catholic schools, and for a brief time
she attended the Model Secondary School for the Deaf at Gallaudet
University. Because of her financial situation she decided not to go
to Gallaudet University. Actually, Kali ended up dropping out of high
school altogether when her mother got sick. After her mother died, Kali
enrolled in the GED program at Stanhope College. Her success and
enjoyment in that program influenced her to continue at Stanhope for
her college basics. She is currently living with her sister while she com-
pletes her general education requirements and prepares to transfer to a
four-year institution. She is considering California State University at
Northridge and Northern Illinois University, both of which have well-
regarded programs for deaf students. For her major she is thinking of
business, pharmacy, or education.

Kali was attending tutoring for the second semester of the freshman
sequence, Rhetoric 102, which focuses on writing about literature. In
the fall semester she took the first course in the sequence. In an interview,
Kali discussed her attitude about writing:

> I wanna write, I wanna write well. I know before I came here to the
> school I never wrote. I didn't write much at all. And I didn't . . . I did
> read a lot, but I didn't write a lot. So I didn't have confidence in my
> writing ability. But now this is my first year experiencing writing and
> doing essays, everything. So, I wrote an essay in high school, but it
> was nothing like what I'm doing here. Still, I withdrew from school,
> and I missed out on so much. And everything in the English course.
> And that's why I didn't have a lot of experience until I came here
> to Stanhope College. And so I've had good experiences and chal-
> lenges, and it's exciting, too. I really love it. I love to write. Before,
> I didn't have any idea how to write or have anybody to help me
> with this. And now with the tutoring, it's helped me so much. So, it's

been good. I hope that I can continue to write more 'cause I really love writing. And I learn how to be more confident in the writing. Before, I didn't like to show people my writing because I only knew one way. I know that the only way I really can improve my writing is to show people my writing and get different points of view. And to change some of my writing and work on my weak areas.

Gustav, her tutor, said that she was a special tutee because of her talent and her attitude. Like Rae, she is especially motivated and takes control of her own learning. For instance, she makes it a point to tell the interpreter or tutor what she needs, and if it's not working out, she asks to work with someone else. She valued learning about writing in the tutoring sessions, and she was interested in more than just grammar. In fact, she valued learning about research, paragraphing, development, essay structure, and focus. She also appreciated the clear, specific feedback she got in the writing center.

CHAPTER 2

⌒

The Research Context

T HE CONCEPT OF insider/outsider status is complex: "A single body cannot bridge that mythical divide between insider and outsider, researcher and researched. I am neither, in any simple way, yet I am both" (Weston, quoted in Olesen 2000, 227). Like Weston, as a researcher, I am both. I am an insider as a writing center person but an outsider to the actual tutorial relationship and to Deaf culture. Rubin and Rubin (1995) write that one way to gain insider status is to learn the language of those whom one is studying; for that reason, I have completed Level I and Level II sign language classes at the Center for Sight and Hearing in Rockford, IL.

Neal Lerner (1996) also studied writing center tutors with ethnographic methods. Many of his observations are similar to mine. Seemingly, writing center theory is based on ideas from other fields that are applied to writing centers. North asks, "What happens in writing tutorials?" (1984b, 29). Lerner puts this idea into practice by recording tutoring sessions and interviewing participants. He focuses mainly on the tutors' experiences, however. In contrast, I provide the viewpoints of all participants. Lerner finds that one of the key conflicts in tutoring is the tension between the tutors' focus on process, the tutees' desire to get their texts fixed, and the writing center's reluctance to be seen as a fix-it shop. In my study, the writing center does not take on this kind of identity. I find that the main focus is the larger give-and-take between tutors and tutees, who have somewhat different goals and expectations for the sessions. These objectives relate to literacy, entering a discourse community, and enforcing that community's expectations.

While conducting the study I tried to remain flexible with my research methods. When I arrived at one of the research sites for the first interview, I realized I had forgotten my tape recorder, so I had to borrow one. After videotaping the first tutoring session, one of the deaf participants (Rae), the interpreter (Linda), and I began our first audio-taped interview with a borrowed recorder. As we were talking, I noticed that the "record" light was not on. When I bent down and turned up the volume, the light went on. When I tried to transcribe the tape, the beginning was so faint that I could not hear it. The first part of the interview had been lost. I found it ironic that the inability to hear would affect my data collection. We had discussed videotaping the interview, but I was too invested in my original plan to change.

Finally, after the second interview, Rae suggested that I videotape the interviews. She explained that a deaf person is not represented on an audiotape—only the interpreter's voice is there—so I took her advice and videotaped our third interview and subsequent interviews with another deaf tutee, Blue. Deaf study participant Kali declined to give her permission to be videotaped. I had not planned to videotape the interviews with deaf participants since I am not fluent in sign language, and I did not expect there would be any relevant nonlinguistic visual data. I also fully trusted the interpreters to accurately voice the deaf tutees' words. I see now that I was both insensitive and naïve in not planning to videotape the interviews with the deaf participants. The drawback to the videotaped interviews is that the audiotaped interviews, when recorded at the proper level, are easy to transcribe, while transcribing videotaped interviews is extremely tedious. In the end, the videotaped interviews did not produce any extra usable data, but again, this is probably due to my rudimentary signing skills and my reliance on the interpreters for the deaf participants' words and meanings. I did notice some facial expressions and gestures on the tapes, but I had already noted these in the observations.

Methods in Grounded Theory

The primary research methods employed were naturalistic observation and semistructured interviews. Other methods were general observation of context and collection of related documents such as student papers, handouts, and writing center materials. I also verified any other observations and tentative conclusions with the participants in the interview sessions and by means of participant feedback on drafts. This member-checking procedure, or participant feedback (Lincoln and Guba 1985), is a common verifying practice in qualitative research. After each field visit I wrote a field memo of my objective experience and a journal entry noting my subjective reactions. As I coded the data I wrote coding and analytic memos. In the final report, I use *thick description* (Ryle 1971) to describe the case, which contains a detailed narrative and excerpts of actual sessions so that readers can experience what I did and draw their own conclusions (Stake 2000).

Data were collected in a ten-month period, during which twenty-eight field visits were made to four different colleges. Only two of these colleges produced sufficient data to be included in the final data set. The data were not consistently collected during this time but rather were gathered in fits and spurts and at the mercy of the various colleges' academic calendars. For instance, I was unable to collect data during the summer months. The two sites that yielded the final usable data were a writing center in a four-year private college in a major Midwestern city and an academic assistance center in a community college in a suburb of the same city. The main data consist of nineteen tutoring sessions, thirty-six interviews, and various written documents.

Observation

The qualitative data collection consisted primarily of observations of tutoring sessions. In addition, I videotaped or audiotaped tutoring sessions and interviews. The choice of video- or audiotape depended on the hearing status of the interlocutor and that person's preference. For instance, I audiotaped interviews with hearing people, but after deaf participant Rae's advice, I attempted to videotape interviews with deaf people, unless the participant objected. The video- and audiotapes enabled me to confirm my observations and to transcribe not only the exact text of the sessions but also other aspects such as the physical setup of the tutoring area, the seating arrangements of the participants, and the content and negotiation of focus for the tutoring session. The tutoring sessions focused on writing (e.g., topic generation), revising for higher- or lower-order concerns, actual composing, reflecting on what was written, or information work, such as reading comprehension and research.

The data also consist of the communication model used, such as sign language interpreter, written notes, or computer. I noted observations of the interpersonal dimension as I perceived it and verified my interpretations later with the participants. In this way, I triangulated any "contestable description" by verifying my interpretation with that of the participants and carefully describing what I saw and the reasons for my interpretation (Stake 1995). I observed two to five tutorials with each of the six participants (three deaf and three hearing), which resulted in the observation of eighteen tutoring sessions and one extra audiotaped session. I videotaped the tutoring sessions (with the exception of deaf study participant Kali, who declined permission to videotape, as stated earlier); in her case, I audiotaped the tutoring sessions. In addition to observing specific tutoring sessions, I made general observations of the writing center layout, physical location, and context.

Interviews

Semistructured interviews with stakeholders were a main source of data, along with general observations of the context. First, I confirmed my observations of the session with the participants. Then I asked them to give their feedback on the effectiveness of the session, including problems or good points, and to describe their feelings about working together. I tried to respect the tutee's communication preference and offered to conduct the interviews via email, with an interpreter, through speech, or however the student preferred. All of the deaf students in the study preferred to conduct the interview through an interpreter, and I recorded them either on audio- or videotape. Once I had a chance to interview one of the deaf participants without an interpreter, but I declined because my signing skills are too rudimentary. All of the interviews with the hearing participants were audiotaped. Since the interviews with the deaf participants were conducted through an interpreter, it is the interpreter's voice rather than the tutee's on the tape; therefore, the reader needs to keep in mind that any quotes from the deaf participants are an interpretation of their meaning, not necessarily their exact words.

Also, through member checking (participant feedback) of transcripts, the deaf and the hearing participants had an opportunity to correct the interpreter's words in case of a misinterpretation or a researcher's error in transcription. I also interviewed the interpreters, center directors, and other stakeholders, such as the disabilities services director, to get additional views of the process. I tried to interview the key participants after each tutoring session, and when this proved inconvenient, I attempted to interview them as soon as possible—preferably within two days—so the session would still be fresh in their minds. All of the participants were interviewed at least once and had follow-up interviews in person or by phone, email, or regular mail. For instance, when going over the transcripts, if I had a specific question, I contacted the participants by email or regular mail, or I called them. I transcribed and coded the interview data for emergent concerns, from both the participants' and outsiders' points of view. These codes focus on describing fully and accurately the dynamic of each session and of the tutoring relationship in general.

Written Documents

I collected written documents relating to the tutoring session and writing center context where available. If, as Gail Wood (1995) has recommended, tutorials had been conducted via a word-processing program on a computer, then I could have saved the documents and studied the transcripts later. The difference between Wood's tutorial and other electronic tutorials is that her technique has both tutor and tutee sitting side by side at the same computer. The computer screen is used only as a quicker substitute for written notes. So, the only difference is the writing medium: keyboard and screen versus pencil and paper. Unfortunately, I was not able to observe any tutorials conducted in this manner. I did, however, collect the written notes used in the one session that was conducted that way, but since the participant did not want to continue in the study, this session was not included in the final data set for analysis. I also gathered related documents, as Stake (1995) recommends, including tutor-training materials, writing center publicity, tutor log entries, discarded written notes used in the conference, and the actual texts writers worked on during the conference.

Unusable Data

Unfortunately, about a third of the data I collected were unusable for the study because they did not meet the criteria for inclusion. For this, I needed to observe two or more tutoring sessions with a deaf student at a particular research site, and I excluded hard of hearing students as presenting different issues. Observation of only one tutoring session is not enough to make an analysis, as any one tutoring session in isolation cannot be contextualized and could be an anomaly. I also included only interviews that were associated with the minimum of two observations. Hence, two interviews I conducted with administrators were unusable since no formal tutoring observations resulted at those institutions. At one potential research site I observed one tutoring session with Sarah, who I did not know was hard of hearing until after the observation (the writing center director had said she was deaf), and one with Tom, who declined further observations, so those observations could not be included. In all, I had five research sites that gave me permission to research, twelve informed consent forms signed by participants, four interviews, and two observations of tutoring sessions that could not be included in the data set.

Final Data Set

The formal data set consists of observations of tutoring sessions, interviews, and related documents at two institutions. The audio- and video-tapes were transcribed and member-checked, resulting in approximately five hundred pages of raw data involving sixteen participants, nineteen tutoring session observations, and thirty-six interviews (see table 1). I also collected related documents such as the papers students were working on, tutor-training materials, writing center publicity materials, and tutor-training materials at both colleges.

Data Coding and Analysis Procedures

The primary methodology was the grounded-theory approach (Strauss and Corbin 1998). In grounded theory, the researcher allows relevant concepts to emerge from the data and in turn is guided by these emergent concepts in further data collection and analysis. In other words, I allowed the codes, concepts, and theories to emerge as I studied the data (Strauss and Corbin 1998; Charmaz 2000).

I analyzed the observation and interview data by first transcribing and then coding the transcripts. I transcribed in entirety the first round of videotaped tutoring sessions and the audio- and videotaped interviews. After reading over transcripts and marking codes, I wrote coding memos outlining the insight I gained and the questions that still needed to be answered. I also represented the codes textually and graphically to help me further understand their relationships both to each other and to the greater study. Then I engaged in axial coding and finally wrote the story of the research. As I transcribed the tapes of the interviews and tutoring sessions, I kept a log called a codebook of relevant concepts and arranged the codes as I went along. Rather than using predetermined codes, I let the topics emerge from the data, as mentioned earlier. I gathered these codes in constantly evolving text and graphic representations to determine their relationships and create wider categories. I used open and axial coding, as well as analytic memos, to keep track of the unfolding patterns and concerns (Strauss and Corbin 1998). While looking for relevant patterns, and as Stake recommended, I spent more time on interesting and relevant passages from interviews and tutoring session transcripts, attempting to resist easy interpretations and searching instead for deeper meanings. These techniques are similar to those recommended by Maxwell (1996), such as letting categories become apparent from my analytic memos and participants' concerns (emic concerns). I also attempted to use *in vivo* codes, which are codes derived from the words and phrases that the participants used during their tutoring work and interviews (Strauss and Corbin 1990).

As the interviews are a form of negotiated text, I reconfirmed these emerging topics with participants in subsequent interviews. I also compared tutoring practices used in the sessions with those stressed in training and delved into the tutoring techniques associated with the theories they are overtly or covertly based on. As Strauss and Corbin recommended, I then thought about the data as a whole and asked, "What is going on here?" Specifically, they recommend asking, "What is the main issue or problem with which these people seem to be grappling? What keeps striking me over and over? What comes through, although it might not be said directly?" (1998, 148). The answer turned out to be literacy or the desire to enter a new discourse community and to acquire the required skills to do so. I then related the subcategories to this main category by asking, "What happens in the tutorial?" Specifically, I asked, (1) "What is the content of the tutoring session? (2) How is tutoring accomplished? and (3) What are the other contributing factors?"

The goal of my data analysis is to tell the story of specific practices and themes in tutorials that involve hearing tutors and deaf tutees. As a result, I make recommendations for tutor training and tutoring practice. The choice of these themes was guided by my primary research question, which is concerned with what happens in a tutorial between a deaf tutee and a hearing tutor. More particular concerns focused on the content of the session, how the tutoring was conducted, what communication model was used, and other factors such as feelings, interpersonal relationships, and culture. First I describe each theme or concept based on my observations, field notes, analytic memos, and transcripts. I explain commonalties and differences between and among cases, as well as use direct interpretation from observation (Stake 1995).

Generally I looked for (a) the topics that were covered and the techniques that were used in the tutorial, (b) the communication factors that were involved, and (c) the general dynamic of the session. I assumed I would see only small differences between what deaf and hearing students learned in the tutorial, and the data confirmed this. I saw work on revision, both higher- and lower-order concerns (Reigstad and McAndrew 1984), the writing process (e.g., composing and idea generation), and the gathering and understanding of information. I anticipated seeing rhetorical expectations (the interplay between what the writer would offer and what the reader would expect from a paper) as a likely factor, and this was realized in the tutors' adherence to the teachers' objectives. I expected to find differences in deaf students' writing processes and rhetorical expectations, as Margaret Weaver (1996) did. I thought it likely that editing and proofreading would be issues since deaf students' writing often contains errors and tutors are sometimes trained not to proofread. This may cause uneasiness or even guilt on the tutor's part when editing a deaf student's paper (Blau, Hall, and Sparks 2002) or frustration on the tutee's part if the tutor refuses to give editing help. I predicted that tutors would use visual means of communication, especially writing, and, if so, this might cause uneasiness for the tutor, as many tutors are trained not to write anything for the student, but this was not apparent in the study data. Interpretation from sign language to English is a main factor, and I expected to see various ways of negotiating meaning and textual modeling both through an interpreter and in writing, which I did. Since, as mentioned earlier, Deaf culture values direct communication, common "hands-off" tutoring practices (Chappell 1982; Brooks 1991) may create confusion or even a breakdown of the session. I also anticipated that tutors would modify their normal tutoring practices to meet the deaf students' needs.

In addition to the grounded-theory approach to the overall understanding of the phenomena, I analyze important stretches of tutoring dialogue using the ideas in Kutz (1997). I chose passages that illustrate a salient point, were discussed in the interviews, or that puzzled or interested me during the coding sessions.

INTERLUDE

───✦

Hearing Tutees

Squirt

Squirt is twenty-one years old, white, and hearing. She is also a lesbian, and this identity is extremely important to her. She has a specific learning disability that affects her receptive and expressive language abilities. She chose her unusual pseudonym because she wanted to be named after her cat. Her cat's name is Squirt, but I misheard it as Sport. I thought "Sport" would be a good name for her since she is a big basketball fan. But when I told her that her name would be "Sport," which I quite liked, she said she wanted her name to be "Pussy" instead. Perhaps her learning disability prevented her from fully thinking through the implications of such a pseudonym. In any event, when I suggested she go back to her original pseudonym, Squirt, she agreed.

Squirt's mother is a former teacher. Both her parents, who met at summer school at Harvard, have master's degrees. Squirt's major at Davis is musical theater performance. She frequently goes to auditions, performs in shows, and records her music, and she keeps me up to date with these activities. Her career goals are to be in show business—films, Broadway performances, dancing, singing, or something similar. Of all of the participants in the study, I identified with Squirt the most, especially with her energy and determination. On her right wrist she wears a watch, indicating lefthandedness.

Squirt had been attending the writing center for years. In fact, her tutor, Newby, called her a "regular." In the semester during which the study was carried out, she was attending tutoring for her gay/lesbian literature class. Squirt stated that she liked all of her tutors and generally had a good experience in the writing center. When I asked her why she had first come to the writing center, she replied, "To get help. To get support. It's very supportive." I asked her what they did to help her there, and she said, "They pushed me . . . to write more. They would give me a lot of ideas to write about." She reflected, "I love to write," but added that sometimes she was frustrated with her tutoring sessions and wished her tutor, in this case Newby, would "explain things more." As an outcome of her tutoring she would like "to become a more confident writer." In an ideal tutoring session she would like the tutor to "give me more feedback . . . about the content . . . I wanna get more tips." She wants to know what the tutor thinks of her paper. Squirt, who has also done some tutoring, described her own technique: "I gave him, like, tips. I told him, like, what he needs to work on, stuff like that. His papers were really short. And I gave him tips on how to make it longer and stuff." Squirt is also a published writer; she writes a youth column for a gay newspaper.

Shareef

Shareef is an eighteen-year-old hearing black man. I noticed that he was very organized, as he kept his computer discs in cases and had all of his papers arranged in folders. He told me how dedicated he was to his studies and that he knows "it's serious now." He stated that he wants to work hard and show his teacher that he cares about his work: "I want to give her the best stuff I can."

Shareef lives with his foster mother, with whom he grew up. He plans on staying with her until he is financially able to move out. His current job is "flipping burgers." As a young adolescent, Shareef converted to Islam. He credits his faith with showing him the right path and helping him not to get involved with the wrong crowd. He feels that the Muslim faith is more important for the black community than the Christian faith and believes that it has put him on the right track to go to college.

Shareef is a film major at Davis, but he is interested in music writing, production, and performance. Ultimately he would like to be a music engineer. When I met Shareef, he was working on a recording of his rap compositions. In one of his papers he wrote about his desire to become a rapper. He is also interested in making music videos and combining his love of music and film. He is considering changing his major from film to something involving music.

Shareef attended tutoring sessions as part of the requirement for Intro to College Writing, the developmental course at Davis. About his writing he said, "I like writing because I have so much stuff to talk about. But, as far as the grammatical stuff, that's always been my problem, and now in college I'm paying for it. So I have to go back and relearn some stuff, you know. I didn't pay too much attention when I was younger, and now I've gotta go back and learn it." He feels confident when coming to tutoring and appreciates the fact that his tutor, John, is a peer. Like all of the tutees in the study, Shareef is extremely motivated and loves to write. He told me on several occasions, "I love to write." His enthusiasm also showed when, in an interview with me, he discussed his attitude toward writing:

> I love writing. Writing is my favorite subject now. . . . There's so much you can do with writing . . . plus my career is mainly involved in our writing; you're taking a concentration in directing, in filming, you have to do tons of reading, you have to do tons of writing.

Shareef's enthusiasm is contagious and inspiring.

As for his tutor, Shareef feels that John

> has been helping me a lot with my writing and grammatical stuff. . . . He's the one helping me out. . . . I come in with a plan, I need this and that . . . and he just kind of follows my guidelines. . . . I think the main job of a tutor is to guide. Not to do the work but to play a guide . . . [and] to be an open-minded type of person, and that's how [John] is.

When I talked to him, Shareef was getting a feeling of confidence in his writing: "I feel like I've stepped up a little bit from where I used to be. I feel like I'm evolving. That's how I know I'm ready." He said, "I feel confident whenever I come to tutoring. And whenever I leave, my confidence goes up a notch . . . [because I] get motivated to do better."

Herrodrick

Herrodrick, who is eighteen, white, and hearing, comes from a suburban background. In high school he played music and participated in theatrical productions. His parents were out of work for a while, and he and his sister were the only ones working in the household. Currently, his father is a bank teller, and his mother is a nurse.

Herrodrick and his twin sister are both film majors at the college. Herrodrick has been a creative writer since school and is now working on a fantasy/science-fiction novel. He told me that he had started writing in the eighth grade: "The teacher I had really inspired me to be creative and really go about different works and basically put yourself in your writing . . . just throw yourself into your writing, and see where it takes you." He told me about his attitude toward writing in high school: "When I got writing assignments, I'd think 'Okay, here are the boundaries. How can I go to the edge of 'em? Or maybe stay within 'em but make it interesting?'" As a writer, he was surprised when he tested into English Composition I Enhanced (with tutorial component), when his sister, who is not as strong in English as he, tested into the regular English Composition I, and some of his friends tested out of English all together. His attitude was, "Well, at least I'll come out of it even better than before." (The frustration for film students at Davis, as Shareef also explained, is that they are not allowed to take film classes until they finish the basic sequence in English.) Herrodrick is sensitive and thoughtful, and most of his tutoring sessions focused on discussion of his ideas.

His tutor, John, works with him on both his English papers and his creative writing project. John points out grammar issues and encourages Herrodrick to refer to the handbook. They also talk about "different ideas on how to express [Herrodrick's thoughts] on paper and where to throw little sparks and gadgets in, or whatever you call [them], interesting points into the writing itself." John's help inspired Herrodrick to revisit his creative piece, which he had abandoned after receiving disappointing feedback. Herrodrick's notion of a successful tutoring session is one that "you . . . come out [of] . . . feeling . . . more fulfilled in your writing. And once you actually grasp that concept . . . you'll basically build upon your confidence." After the tutoring sessions Herrodrick goes home and jots down notes. He is glad that John is a peer tutor; because of their age similarity John "gives a better perspective" than a teacher because he is "going through the same thing" as other students. In addition, because John is a film major, "we can cover more ground . . . [since I don't have] to explain . . . certain things. . . . John's a great tutor for me." Herrodrick likes that John gives him suggestions but leaves the decisions up to him and that John encourages him to use his creativity when writing about the various topics. Herrodrick especially treasures John's role as a listener.

CHAPTER 3

⁓

Literacy Work in
the Tutoring Session

THE CONTENTS OF a tutoring session are similar regardless of whether the conference involves a deaf student and a hearing tutor or a hearing student and a hearing tutor. In fact, all of the tutoring sessions I observed—for both deaf and hearing tutees—centered around some type of literacy work: writing on the one hand and gathering and understanding information on the other. The traditional writing process is typically broken down into the following steps: prewriting, writing, revising (sometimes editing and proofreading are a separate category), and publishing. The writing tasks I observed, which were only slightly different, consisted of planning, writing, revising, and reflecting:

- Planning is talking about ideas for writing before any text has been produced.
- Writing is composing during the conference, either on a computer or on paper.
- Revising consists of working on higher-order or lower-order concerns.
- Reflecting is talking about the ideas that were written about after the assignment is finished and turned in to the teacher.

Information work consists of both reading and research:

- Reading work is either assistance with or discussion about reading a text for information or summarizing, or for evidence to support a literary analysis.
- Research is actual research using the Internet or a discussion of possible research techniques. (See table 2 for content of the session broken down by tutee.)

All tutoring-session content in this study can be categorized by this system; there may be other content categories that I did not observe or other ways of categorizing the content, but in grounded-theory analysis, decisions have to be made, and these are the categories as I see them.

Although it is difficult to make generalizations from such a small sample, some patterns are immediately apparent. The only area that all six deaf and hearing tutees worked on was revising for lower-order concerns (LOCs). Some tutees spent entire tutoring sessions revising only for LOCs, whereas others only had one or two corrections in all of the sessions I observed. All of the deaf tutees worked on both reading and revising for LOCs, whereas all of the hearing tutees worked on revising for HOCs (higher-order concerns) and LOCs but to different extents.

TABLE 2. *Content of the Tutoring Session*

Tutee	Writing					Information	
	planning	composing	revising HOCs	revising LOCs	reflecting	reading	research
Deaf							
Rae		X	X	X	X	X	X
Blue				X		X	
Kali			X	X		X	X
Hearing							
Shareef		X	X	X			
Herrodrick	X		X	X	X		X
Squirt		X	X	X		X	

In some tutoring sessions it was hard to distinguish between planning, composing, and revising for HOCs since many times these activities were intertwined. I called "composing" any actual writing that was done in the session beyond simple revisions. I limited "planning" to ideas for text that had not yet been generated. I categorized as "revising for HOCs" work on organization, argument, and analysis. I categorized as "revising for LOCs" work on word choice and punctuation. In the following sub-sections, I discuss the tutees in the order in which they appear in table 2.

Writing Work

In a writing tutorial, it should be no surprise that people worked on writing. What may be surprising was that reading and research were also covered. I discovered this while coding data, as I did not impose an external structure on the data but let the categories emerge from it. Through my grounded-theory analysis, I found a logical way to break down the writing work: planning what to write, actual composing in the tutoring session, revising for higher- and lower-order concerns, and reflecting on what one had written. Although these steps somewhat resemble the classic process categories of prewriting, writing, revising, and publishing, they grew organically out of the data. Reflecting on what was written appears to be a category unique to this study. Breaking down the revising into HOCs and LOCs was natural because it was apparent from the data that these were two different activities—even though tutor and tutee can alternate between them in a given session; they also appear to be an established category in writing center methodology.

Planning

I differentiated planning from other activities since it involved talking about a text that was not yet written rather than revising an existing text. Herrodrick, a hearing student, was the only tutee I observed planning. He spent two of the three sessions I observed talking about his ideas rather than revising a text. He was also the only participant who spent entire sessions talking about ideas. All of the other sessions I observed concentrated at least part of the time on revising an existing text. The second session I observed with Herrodrick concentrated solely on the assignment sheet. He and his tutor, John, spent the entire time talking about ideas for Herrodrick's paper. The free-flowing conversation resembled a discussion between friends rather than a formal tutoring session.

First, John read the assignment aloud, and then they began discussing ideas for a paper. They talked about what Herrodrick would not write about: cliché topics like abortion or the legalization of marijuana or anything too broad. John suggested that he choose a topic he was passionate about. Herrodrick reflected on some cultural observations he had made, like how people do not talk to each other on the train. From here they started discussing the differences between country and city, and Herrodrick paused to take some notes on the conversation. As they collaborated, John repeated the theme as a possible topic: "That seems like an interesting paper. 'Why do people move to big cities?' That seems like a stable enough premise for a paper." As the discussion continued, John brought the conversation back to the beginning and anchored it to the idea of topic generation. Then, he asked Herrodrick for more information while he took notes. John ended the session with a recap:

> That's the best way to do it . . . just talk about whatever comes to mind even if some things don't seem related . . . And then get . . . a basic premise for your paper, and then cut off the fat. Condense it and make it more specific. Sometimes instead of going specific, instead of just picking something specifically, sometimes you don't know, exactly. All right, this is great.

Any planning that was done in other sessions was based on some finished writing, which I categorized under "revising for HOCs."

Composing

Composing is extended writing that takes place in the tutorial session; it does not include simple note taking. Composing happens when the tutor or the tutee wants to capture an idea that has been generated and add it immediately to the text, either on paper or on the computer. Rae composed on the computer, and Shareef and Squirt composed on paper. John seemed to want Shareef, a hearing student, to compose on the computer, but after John set him up with one, Shareef wrote by hand instead. Shareef said that he preferred writing by hand and then transferring it to the computer: "I just prefer to do it by hand when the idea's fresh in my head. I gotta write it down." John said that in every tutoring session they would talk about Shareef's paper, and then he would give Shareef time to write, about twenty minutes per session. John explained: "Shareef I have write every session, just because there's always . . . an abundance of ideas that . . . he has . . . so I want him to get it on the page immediately." John went on to explain that other students sometimes have trouble generating ideas, whereas Shareef always has plenty of ideas and needs to write them down right away. They did this only in the first session I observed, however. I had supposed that, because I was there, they thought twenty minutes of composing would not be interesting for me to observe, but John later told me that he did not consciously alter his tutoring practices because of my presence.

Rae, a deaf student, also worked with John and did some composing during their tutoring session. Of the three sessions I observed with Rae and John, two were focused on doing research on the Internet, and one was spent revising a paper for her Spanish history class. Rae had her paper on a disk, and they looked it over on a computer. As they came up with ideas, Rae would add them right into the paper. This is different from revising for HOCs in that the writing was actually done during the tutoring session. It was Rae's idea that she compose. She and John were talking about the questions for the assignment when she said, "Let's switch spots," because she wanted to type her ideas into the computer right away. John and Rae were actually collaborating on the keyboard. At one point John commented, "It's hard to type with one hand over here," and Rae responded, "You can tell me and I can type." A little while later Rae typed while John read what she typed and then commented on it. As they composed, they also revised. Later, they switched to pen and paper, and John took notes as Rae generated ideas; Rae remarked, "It works better that way." This technique of the student typing text directly into the computer for the tutor to read seems especially effective for deaf students. Rae explained:

> I was telling John what to do, and he was doing that [typing] for me, and then I felt like it would probably have been better if I was just

typing it for myself. . . . And . . . having him sit there in a different position once we switched, it was better [because] I could just type it out and see what was going on in my mind . . . and he could easily look over at the screen and make the changes that needed to be made with the grammar, punctuation—instead of me telling him what to do. . . . It just makes more sense.

Of course it makes more sense for the deaf tutee to directly compose on the computer so the tutor can see the English rather than asking a question, receiving an answer in sign language, and having it interpreted, and then the student still has to write it down in English. Composing directly saves a step, and the tutee also gets practice composing directly into English.

With Squirt, a hearing tutee, and Newby, her tutor, both sessions I observed focused on Squirt's paper about *Giovanni's Room*, a novel by James Baldwin. In the first session, as Newby read through the paper, Squirt would be prompted to write, and she would write right there and then. Similar to Rae's process, instead of answering Newby's questions aloud, Squirt would turn to the paper and write the responses, adding to her text. When the tutee responds to the tutor's question aloud, the response has to be remembered and written later. Writing the response immediately saved a step for Squirt, a hearing student, as it did with Rae, a deaf student. For example, in this exchange, Squirt responded to Newby's questions by writing, sometimes talking at the same time, and then Newby got the response by reading what Squirt had written:

Newby: He was seeing Giovanni, but they didn't have sexual relations, is that what you're saying?

Squirt: They probably did. I'm sure they did. Yeah, they did. [writing]

Newby: [puts on glasses, takes book, looks at it]

Squirt: Yeah, they did. Now I remember. I remember they, like, slept together.

Newby: And he was also having a sexual relationship with a woman, Hella, right? [continues to look at book]

Squirt: [writing] Yeah, yeah. [finishes writing]

Newby: So, what was—let me see what you wrote.

This pattern of collaboration and writing continued throughout this tutoring session and the next one: Newby guided Squirt, and she wrote.

The difference between composing and revising in the tutoring session is that is the former entails sustained attention to writing for at least a minute. The latter requires only a word or two or a quick note about what to add, but there is no extended composing of new material. Nevertheless, this composing *is* revising for HOCs because the tutee is adding to an existing text. Other than Shareef's writing time, I did not observe any composing of new text as in freewriting or responding to a writing prompt, but I would also classify this activity as composing rather than planning, which is limited to discussing ideas.

Revising

Higher-order concerns are those points that "are central to the meaning and communication of the piece . . . matters of thesis and focus, development, structure and organization, and voice" (McAndrew and Reigstad 2001, 42), while LOCs are "matters related to surface appearance, correctness, and standard rules of written English" (56). I have used this definition and the overall concept of HOCs and LOCs that first appeared in Reigstad and McAndrew's *Training Tutors for Writing Conferences* (1984), a highly influential, seminal writing center text, because the concept is traditionally accepted by writing center scholars even though LOCs are sometimes called later-order concerns (Blau et al. 2001; Blau, Hall, and Sparks 2002; Gillespie and Lerner 2003; Harris 1986; various discussions on Wcenter) and also because the data bear it out. These concerns are also known as global and local concerns. In chapter 4 I use the concepts of finding and correcting errors for the techniques involved in working with LOCs, and in the conclusion I use the concepts of editing and proofreading to combine both the content category of LOCs and the techniques of finding and correcting of errors.

I present the students' revising concerns in table 3 (higher-order concerns) and table 4 (lower-order concerns). I arrange them by tutee in order to show the tutee's concerns as a whole, which may lead the reader to a greater understanding of these students' individual needs as writers. Since HOC and LOC revisions are never discrete in the tutoring session,

TABLE 3. *Higher-Order Concerns by Tutee*

Tutees	Higher-Order Concerns				
	thesis/ focus	assignment	development	organization	rhetorical diction
Deaf					
Rae		X	X		
Blue					
Kali	X	X	X		
Hearing					
Squirt	X	X	X	X	
Shareef	X	X	X		
Herrodrick	X	X			X

sometimes discussions overlap. Nevertheless, the reader should get a good idea of the revising concerns for each tutee in the study.

Higher-Order Concerns

All of the tutees but Blue worked on higher-order concerns in their writing at some point. The revision process varied somewhat according to the particular tutoring dyad.

Deaf Tutees.   Rae brought in a paper that she was working on to her tutoring session with John. She loaded it on the computer and asked him to read it:

> So, what I'd like you to do is just to check out my paper, just to . . . make sure it makes sense. I'm not totally finished with it. I do have a lot more to go, but I'd like to get your feedback about what I should do next, what more information I should add to it.

While reading the paper, John moved back and forth between higher- and lower-order concerns, much like Rae herself did in saying what she wanted him to attend to. These concerns included editing, checking her paper for clarity, and suggesting what she should add to it. John started by doing a little editing for LOCs, then moved to Rae's understanding of the book she was writing about. He then began asking her the questions on the teacher's assignment sheet and encouraged her to answer all of them. At one point Rae asked to switch positions and began answering the questions by typing directly into the computer. She also asked him to look over her notes, and they switched again—this time John asked her questions from the assignment, and as she answered in sign language he took notes so she could add her responses to the text later. Clearly, the tutoring session focused chiefly on expanding and developing the text.

With the help of her tutor, Kali also expanded and developed a text. She came to the tutoring session with the introduction to her paper on Ray Bradbury, and then she and Gustav planned a way to approach the rest of the paper. After reading the introduction, Gustav asked about the assignment. After Kali explained it, Gustav guided her through her approach to the topic and gave her advice about what to include in the paper. This was similar to the session between John and Rae except that Rae was farther along in her composition and revised mostly on-screen. Like John, Gustav began reading Kali's paper with an eye to the content but got distracted by editing concerns. Curiously enough, both tutors were distracted by missing commas with nonrestrictive elements.

Gustav gave Kali a lot of advice about what should be in the paper. They planned what she was going to do with it but did not do any actual composing. Again, development was the HOC focus. In a later tutoring session on this same paper, Gustav read it through first for editing concerns. When Kali said, "It just seems like it's needing something . . . I need to write more to cover everything that's in the paper," Gustav turned back to higher-order issues of thesis and development. He discussed the various parts of the paper and suggested what she might change; for instance, he said, "So there's a little bit here that you might, depending on the length requirement, keep or pitch. OK?" He also encouraged her to expand her ideas into a third main point (the paper currently had only two). He guided her fairly directly on how to revise:

> I would incorporate a couple more of those in either this paragraph or one additional paragraph. But solely on how they relate to mass culture. Nothing else. . . . And just keep the focus on mass culture. So,

whatever you do with the rest of this paragraph here, try to fit it in somewhere else. Don't keep it—you don't have to throw it out, but don't keep it in the same paragraph.

This tutoring session's HOCs were thesis, development, and focus. Gustav's technique is different from John's in that it is more directive.

Hearing Tutees.   Shareef, Herrodrick, and Squirt all revised for HOCs. For Squirt's paper on *Giovanni's Room*, her tutor, Newby, encouraged her to get organized and stay focused. Newby urged Squirt to be specific and to meet the reader's expectations. Squirt constantly assumed in her paper that the reader had read the book. She said at one point, "[The teacher] knows the book more than I do." This was true, but this type of literary analysis calls for the writer to give enough information about the book so that someone who has not read it will understand the essay. So, most of the tutoring session involved Newby encouraging Squirt to put examples from the book into her essay and to give her own interpretation of the story. In these sessions Newby and Squirt seemed extremely contentious, but both claimed that they had a good relationship. Newby had to push Squirt to get her to analyze the text and refer to it explicitly in her argument. Newby told me that, despite being gay, Squirt was reluctant to engage the topics in the gay/lesbian literature class she was taking. In the process of member-checking, Squirt read this comment and disagreed with Newby's analysis, pointing out that she often writes about gay issues both for class and for the local gay paper. In the tutoring session, Newby used Socratic questioning, but Squirt resisted:

> Newby: Why didn't David show his feelings? Why didn't Giovanni
>   know that David cared about him?
> Squirt: Um, [still writing] um, well [unintelligible].
> Newby: Why didn't David let Giovanni know?
> Squirt: Oh, 'cause he was guilty.
> Newby: Guilty of what?
> Squirt: Guilty of loving him.
> Newby: I don't understand that. I don't understand that statement.
> Squirt: You know what I mean.

Newby: No, I don't.
Squirt: Yeah, you do.
Newby: No, I don't. Honestly, I don't know what you're saying.

Most of the two tutoring sessions I observed between Newby and Squirt involved Newby trying to draw her out and urging her to make her arguments explicit and referenced to the text. Squirt's HOCs were mostly development and analysis and making her argument explicit.

Although Shareef's focus was usually on revising for LOCs, his tutor, John, guided him through some expansion and focusing of his ideas. For instance, John pointed out to Shareef that his paper was focused on two different topics and that he should choose just one and concentrate on it:

> If you wanna write about writing and about your skills as a writer, then make the foundation of the paper about writing. That should be the core of the paper. Everything you have should revolve around that. Everything that you say should . . . be relevant in some way to your writing. If you want to . . . make it performing, then you have to switch it all around and . . . have everything . . . revolve around that.

Thesis assignment and focus are the main HOC topics for Shareef. He and John also talked about developing the paper and expanding Shareef's ideas. All of the other revision foci for Shareef were LOCs.

Herrodrick had one tutoring session that focused on revision. He had a draft of a paper analyzing a TV commercial for Trix cereal. His teacher had already made formative comments on the draft, but he had not yet turned it in for a final grade. Herrodrick and John read through the paper and discussed the teacher's comments and ideas for developing the paper to meet the teacher's expectations. John reinforced the ideas the teacher had written in the comments and encouraged Herrodrick to revise the paper accordingly. They discussed his argument and the arrangement of ideas. Herrodrick read his paper aloud, and John commented on the content rather than the form. They actually got into revising for focus when John suggested Herrodrick omit some unrelated material. They went on to work on tone, voice, and proper rhetorical word choice. Herrodrick was the only tutee in the study who explicitly worked on voice and word choice as a rhetorical strategy. At the end of the tutoring session they reviewed the structure of the paper. The HOCs Herrodrick worked on were focus, organization, voice, and development.

Lower-Order Concerns

All of the dyads worked on LOCs—some extensively, some only briefly. I have chosen to detail the tutees' concerns arranged by tutee, both so the reader can get a full understanding of the individual students' concerns, and to stress the tutee as a person rather than to stress the concerns themselves (see table 4). For deaf students in particular, editing and proofreading are significant issues.

Deaf Tutees.   Rae asked John to edit her paper, let her know if it made sense, and tell her if she needed to add anything. John had to read one of the sentences seven times in order to understand it—because the commas were missing in a nonrestrictive clause. The ensuing exchange took up almost three pages of transcript. I believe the problem was with paraphrasing. At times the tutor would get confused by a deaf student's attempt at paraphrasing and have to read a sentence over and over.

I sense that deaf students have a problem with paraphrase, but I have no concrete evidence from the present study. Barnes (2006) however, finds

TABLE 4. *Lower-Order Concerns by Tutee*

Tutees	Lower-Order Concerns				
	grammar	punctuation	word choice	mechanics★	style
Deaf					
Rae		X		X	X
Blue	X	X	X	X	
Kali	X	X		X	X
Hearing					
Squirt	X	X			
Shareef	X	X	X	X	X
Herrodrick		X			

★ Mechanics: capitalization, underlining, use of sources, and so on.

that deaf students have problems with quotations and references. Another interesting thing is that, when John worked on editing concerns with tutees, he apologized or excused himself before and after mentioning LOC issues: "I don't want to focus too much on grammar." At another point when Rae was typing, John reminded her that she needed to capitalize something. They also talked about underlining (or italicizing on the computer) the titles of books and eliminating unnecessary words. It is interesting that John and Rae focused on the use of commas to set off a nonrestrictive element, which Kali and Gustav also concentrated on, and this was the sole LOC that Herrodrick and John discussed in the three tutoring sessions I observed.

Of the five tutoring sessions I observed with Blue, three were line-by-line read-throughs of written pieces to correct surface errors. The pattern was similar in each session: Newby would read a bit and prompt Blue to correct her error. After a few tries, if Blue did not succeed, Newby would supply the answer:

> Newby: OK, here's what I'm reading. "Janet was the youngest nine children in her family." So, a word, one word is missing. "Janet was the youngest."
>
> Blue: In?
>
> Newby: "Janet was the youngest"—between these two.
>
> Blue: Ninth? Should be "the ninth"?
>
> Newby: Janet was the youngest nine children.
>
> Blue: In nine? She was in?
>
> Newby: [Shakes head] That's not it. Let's try "of." "She was the youngest of nine"? Make sense? The youngest of nine?

Often Blue would immediately understand what was needed and correct it right on the paper:

> Newby: [reads] "She was four year old." How many years?
>
> Blue: -s [fixes it]

The types of LOCs Blue worked on were missing or wrong prepositions, verb tense, missing or wrong verbs, missing inflections on possessives and plurals, missing capital letters, idioms, missing or unnecessary articles, pronoun reference, general word choice, word forms (parts of speech), punctuation, and potential interference from Deaf culture and language.

During Blue's tutoring session, two moments in a discussion about LOCs could have been influenced by deafness, Deaf culture, or manual language. When Blue and Newby were going through Blue's presentation on Janet Jackson, Newby found a word that Blue had obviously copied from a source without knowing its meaning. This exchange is worth quoting at length because it aptly illustrates issues of vocabulary, schema (framework of previous knowledge), and attitude:

1   Newby: [turns the page, reads] Do you know this word? ["culled"]

2   Blue: No. I just got it on the Internet. [laughs]

3   Newby: You shouldn't use words if you don't know the meaning of
4   them.

5   Blue: But I got a B!

6   Newby: What do you think it means from what the sentence says?

7   Blue: Maybe like she's a hard worker?

8   Newby: [takes pen, points to paper] What does she do here? Just
9   tell me. This sentence, when you say "she culled from one
10   album seven top-five singles." What does it mean that she
11   "culled"? In your own words, how would you say that?

12   Blue: That Janet Jackson was dancing. She was doing a lot of hard
13   work.

14   Newby: OK, look. She made an album. She had five singles . . . that
15   went to number one. OK. So, you're saying here she was
16   the first artist in history. So, if you were telling me that she
17   did that, how would you tell me in your own words? [takes
18   off glasses, rubs eyes]

19   Blue: I would just say the same story. I mean, that's just all I know.
20   That she was a dancer and that she worked really hard.

21   Newby: No, no. Tell me about this album where she had five singles
22   that were top five—or five singles that were number one.

23   Blue: OK. [smiles, covers face with hands] I have to copy what you
24   just said, right?

25   Newby: I want you to tell me in your own words. Just tell me . . .
26   sign it for me.

27   Blue: I'm sorry. I don't understand.
28   Newby: I want you to tell me in your own words that Janet Jackson
29   made an album, that she got five number-one singles from
30   the album, and that she was the first artist to ever do that.
31   Blue: OK. She's the best dancer in history so far?
32   Newby: We're not talking about dancing. We're talking about sing-
33   ing. Tell your girlfriend . . . that you write to about Janet
34   Jackson's album. What was the name of it? [puts on glasses,
35   looks at paper] *Rhythm Nation,* I guess. Tell your girlfriend
36   about *Rhythm Nation* and how many singles Janet Jackson
37   had. Just tell your girlfriend about it.
38   Blue: Guess what! In all of history there are five songs! I don't
39   know. It's hard.
40   Newby: [puts on glasses, shows Blue paper]
41   Blue: I don't understand.
42   Newby: OK. Here. We're going to get you a dictionary and look
43   this word up. [shows her some other things to do] You fix
44   these while I go find a dictionary. [leaves]
45   Newby: [returns, adjusts glasses, shows dictionary]
46   Blue: [looks at dictionary for six seconds]
47   Newby: Do you understand? Could you give me another word
48   instead of this one?
49   Blue: [sits up, looks unsure, shakes head]
50   Newby: You could say she's—
51   Blue: Seems like it was picked from a group? Is that what?
52   Newby: That's what the dictionary said. That she made from one
53   album, what, you get seven top-five singles. But here's the
54   word we're dealing with: "cull." Look at the paper.
55   Blue: Made?
56   Newby: She was the first artist to have made seven top-five singles
57   from one album.
58   Blue: [Nods]

This exchange illustrates various points related to tutoring deaf students.
Blue admitted in an interview that she needed to work on vocabulary and
that currently vocabulary was not her forte. In the preceding exchange

she acknowledged that she had copied a word she did not know, laughed about it, and then defended herself: "I got a B!" (lines 2 and 5). Newby then encouraged Blue to put the sentence in question into her own words. However, as a deaf girl, she does not listen to Janet Jackson's music the same way hearing young people do. She seems to relate to Janet Jackson primarily as a dancer and a hard worker (lines 7, 12, 20, and 31). In line 32 Newby said, "We're not talking about dancing. We're talking about singing," but according to Blue, Janet Jackson is primarily a dancer, not a singer.

When Blue asked, in lines 23 and 24, whether she should copy what Newby had said, we are reminded that in some methods of educating deaf students, students are asked to copy their teacher's production of English (Webster 1986). But that is not what Newby wanted. Newby wanted Blue to put the phrase in her own words, but Blue could not since she did not have the schema. Even when Newby retrieved the dictionary, Blue still could not put the definition in her own words (line 51). Blue told me in an interview that looking words up in a dictionary did not help her because she did not understand the definitions. The end of this exchange is also interesting, as Newby phrased the sentence one more time and Blue simply nodded. Realizing Blue was not going to get it, Newby moved on to the next issue.

Another LOC that Blue worked on appears to be lexical (or morphophonemic) interference from American Sign Language. Just as spoken language lexemes are made up of phonemes and morphemes, signed language lexemes are made up of cheremes (or parameters), which consist of handshape, location, movement, orientation, and nonmanual signals (Valli and Lucas 1992). These parameters are like phonemes in that signs, like spoken words, can share several phonemes/parameters, but a change in one parameter results in a new word or sign (called a *minimal pair*). For instance, the spoken words *bad* and *dad* share two phonemes (/æ/ and /d/), but it is the third phoneme (/b/ and /d/) that creates a new word; similarly, if I tap a 5 handshape (open hand, all five fingers extended) with my thumb on my forehead and my palm facing left, the sign means FATHER; but if I produce the same handshape, orientation, and movement on my chin, the sign means MOTHER. If I do the same thing on my chest, it means FINE. So, in ASL, these signs share three parameters, but the change in location results in different meanings.

In one of her papers, Blue wrote, "Now, the woman who has a red hair with bow holds and green eyes." Newby said she was confused by this and asked Blue to explain. The interpreter said, "Holds. Ponytail holder." As Newby was explaining, Jay, the interpreter, interrupted and said, "I kind of messed up. She didn't say ponytail holder." What Blue had done was sign HOLDS at the back of her head. So, there are two issues here in word choice. One is the defining word, "ponytail," which is necessary in English (in her paper she wrote "bow" to define the type of holder), and the other is the form of the noun "holder" rather than the verb "holds." In ASL verbs and nouns are differentiated by motion. This is one of the few times that I saw concrete evidence of ASL interference in written English.

Deaf tutee Kali worked on a few LOCs in her tutoring sessions. Unlike many other tutors, Gustav worked on LOCs with Kali by going over her paper silently, making written comments, and then reviewing them with her, communicating through the interpreter. In the first tutoring session I observed, Gustav took Kali's paper, marked it, and then began discussing surface features. He mentioned that spaces are used after periods and indicated some errors in punctuation and missing articles. He also pointed out errors in pluralization and capitalization. When Kali asked Gustav for an explanation of definite and indefinite articles, he gave her one. They then moved to the next paper, and Gustav began by asking her about her overall plans for organization, development, and research. He then turned to surface concerns, mentioning redundant words, before returning to organization. In the next tutoring session, Kali brought an explication of a poem. Gustav looked at it and offered her some edits. Here is an example:

> [He is diagonally across from Kali at the table. He turns and holds the paper between them so she can see it, pointing with a pen as he explains.] I would start here: [reads] "Dickinson upholds her morals by being an upright person *who* does good deeds" rather than "and" [Kali had written "and" where Gustav substituted "who"]. OK. You could also change it by saying that "she upholds her morals by being an upright person." Really, you'd have to say "who does good deeds" rather than "and does good deeds." You don't wanna say "and." You wanna say "who" because you're further qualifying "upright person."

Through the interpreter, Gustav went on to give comments on the use of articles, colons, semicolons, modals, verb tenses, and parallelism, as well as the fact that a transitive verb needs an object. In the last tutoring session, Gustav read silently through Kali's paper on Ray Bradbury, paused as he found errors, and explained them. At one point he responded as a reader, saying he did not understand a certain sentence and asking her to explain it. He also mentioned the use of articles, tense, and commas with a nonrestrictive element.

Hearing Tutees.   Squirt worked mostly on HOCs in her sessions, but her tutor, Newby, pointed out a few LOCs. At the beginning of the first session I observed, Newby made a general comment about seeing run-ons but did not point them out or tell Squirt how to fix them. Since she said, referring to the run-ons, "You don't normally do that too much, do you?" she obviously knew Squirt could find and fix them herself. As Newby read she commented: "That's a pretty long sentence, don't you think?" but she did not offer a correction or ask Squirt to provide one. The tutoring sessions with Squirt focused mostly on development, not LOCs, but in the second session I observed, Newby again encouraged Squirt to shorten long sentences. Newby read the paper and made comments on sentences, like suggesting she take out "and" and put in a period to divide a long sentence. Newby also remarked on the use of the subjunctive, and then, as she continued to read, she got caught up in Squirt's argument and abandoned the editing.

Shareef's tutoring sessions were primarily about correcting LOCs. In the first tutoring session I observed, John and Shareef discussed focusing and developing his paper, after which John encouraged Shareef to write. When Shareef had finished, John read what Shareef had written and reminded him to use the past tense and also talked about lexical choice. Lexical choice or diction is one concern that could be categorized as either a higher- or a lower-order concern. I have separated them by lexical choice as either rhetorical choice and voice (higher order) or usage and register (lower order). The word John and Shareef discussed was "played." John suggested that Shareef use the words "substituted for" instead, as the original word was in the wrong register.

In the second session that I observed, Shareef asked John to read his paper aloud. As John did so, Shareef took the paper and made corrections, which had to do with parallelism, pronoun agreement, sentence structure, missing articles, and comma after an introductory phrase. For this last concern, John got out his handbook and showed Shareef an example. John also mentioned the use of punctuation with quotation marks and the use of the plural. John actually stopped and reflected on Shareef's need to focus on plural forms:

> I would say . . . the recurring problem you have most probably would be the plural. Make sure—and that's something, all you have to do is really focus on your writing. 'Cause you know, . . . as soon as I show you the sentence you always get it, which is good. 'Cause you know which ones need to be plural. All you need to do when you go back and write it is really focus.

John continued reading Shareef's paper aloud, stopping to correct apostrophes and verb tenses. Sometimes John mentioned an error and explained it; sometimes Shareef would catch an error before John could mention it; and sometimes John would have Shareef read a particular sentence aloud to catch his own error. In the last session I observed, John read a paper of Shareef's with teacher comments and explained the errors. Then John asked Shareef to take the other paper he had, go through it himself, and correct his own errors. Afterward, John took the paper and checked it. He reminded Shareef not to change things that were already correct, which Shareef would sometimes do, since, as a speaker of a nonstandard dialect, forms that are correct in standard English will seem odd in his dialect, so when encountering forms that seem okay, he sometimes assumed that they needed correction.

Herrodrick worked minimally on LOCs in his tutoring sessions with John. In fact, the only LOC John mentioned in any of the three sessions I observed was a comma with a nonrestrictive element, and this was because the teacher, Brock, had marked it on Herrodrick's paper. John remarked, "This is something that could slip past me. And if Brock hadn't pointed this out, I might not even have noticed this." Earlier John had told Herrodrick, "Grammatically, we don't really have to talk about that. . . . You never really have a recurring grammatical thing that we need to talk about. Your grammar's fine for the most part." This is in marked contrast to the way he works with Shareef, which is mostly on grammar.

Conclusion

Every tutee in the study worked on revising for LOCs, and all of the tutees but Blue worked on both HOCs and LOCs. This is interesting because writing center dogma deemphasizes work on topics such as grammar and punctuation, although all of the participants worked to some extent on punctuation. Some of the tutees worked extensively on LOCs (Blue, Shareef), while some just touched on them (Herrodrick, Squirt). All of the deaf students, who are probably less familiar with the conventions of print, worked on mechanics. Tutors should thus be aware that editing for grammatical correctness will likely be an issue when working with deaf students. All of the hearing students worked on thesis/focus. Kali was the only deaf student who worked on organization, and only Herrodrick worked on rhetorical diction. The hearing tutees as a whole worked on more different sorts of higher-order concerns than the deaf tutees, and the types of LOCs were about equally distributed among deaf and hearing tutees, although the total time spent on LOCs was greater for the deaf tutees, with the exception of Shareef, a hearing nonstandard dialect speaker.

This analysis clearly demonstrates that revising for both higher- and lower-order concerns is an important part of tutoring, and revising, especially for LOCs, should not be left out, deemphasized, or forbidden. Revising for LOCs, or editing and proofreading, is an especially important factor for deaf students. On the other hand, since Blue did not revise at all for higher-order concerns, nor did she revise for style, more attention could be paid to deaf and minority tutees to ensure that all of the concerns are covered, not just grammar, punctuation, and other mechanics.

Reflecting

Reflecting appears to be a unique category in this study, and it may even be unique to John's tutoring style. Of the three students I observed working with John, two of them reflected on what they had previously written and turned in to the teacher. None of the other study participants did this, but from my own experience as a tutor I recall students reflecting on their finished papers.

Herrodrick and Rae both reflected on what they had written. Herrodrick was the only one who spent an entire tutoring session doing so. In the previous session I had observed with John and Herrodrick they had planned and discussed what Herrodrick would write; then, in the next session John asked Herrodrick what he had ended up writing about. Herrodrick got out his notes—he did not have a copy of the paper—and said the following:

> I basically constructed . . . two main points about [the topic]. I basically said that . . . Americans tend to isolate themselves from other people because of either . . . an economic aspect or because of America's history.

The session continued for eight more pages of transcript, with Herrodrick telling John what he had written and the two of them discussing it.

Rae was the only other tutee to reflect. When John asked her to tell him about her paper she said this:

> I typed out the paper and wrote up each of the five questions and answered that for each of the books. And then I also added in some of the stuff that we wrote together, and some of the things that I remember that you and I talked about, and some other things that I wrote down that we had talked about . . . And I also added some of the topics from the book to sort of keep the paper as long as it was supposed to be 'cause I was struggling to get it to its minimum, and I had to make up some stuff and flower it up a bit to add the pages.

Perhaps John as a tutor encouraged this reflection. He said that he usually liked to read the student's paper aloud after it had been submitted, but these cases were exceptions: in Herrodrick's case because he did not bring his paper and in Rae's case, as John explained later in the session:

> I'm not gonna read it now 'cause it's six pages. . . . I'll read it later on, after the session. [to researcher] Usually, too, I read in the session.

Sometimes when they come in with their papers I usually read them out loud. But . . . I don't want to read six pages in silence. Especially because she already turned it in. [to Rae] But I'll save it and read it later, and we can talk about it next week.

Shareef, John's other tutee, did not reflect on his finished papers. Rather, when a paper was finished, they would move on to the next assignment or continue to work on issues of grammar and usage in the finished paper.

Information Work

I was naïvely surprised to find that tutorial sessions in writing did not always focus on writing. All of the deaf/hearing tutoring dyads had sessions that centered around information work of some kind. Of the hearing tutees, Squirt's and Herrodrick's sessions concentrated on information work, which I broke down into reading and research. The former consists of reading a text together and attempting to extract meaning by summarizing, paraphrasing, analyzing, or explicating. Research consists of doing or learning about actual research, for instance, looking something up on the Internet or talking about research techniques, resources, ideas, or possibilities.

Reading

All of the deaf tutees had tutoring sessions that focused on reading, and Squirt, the only hearing student with a learning disability in the study, also had tutoring sessions that concentrated on reading. Rae discussed reading in her tutoring session with John. They did not do a lot of reading as some dyads did, but they discussed the reading that she had to do for the paper she was writing and actually read from the book at one point. Rae had to read two books and write a paper on them. She admitted that one of the books was difficult for her:

Rae: The problem for me is I'm having trouble understanding the book. . . . It's hard to kind of take information from it and figure out who's who. . . . So, in class we talked about the book, and at that point I started to understand more about the book. But I don't have a real in-depth idea of what it's about. I just have a surface idea.

John: What's the main problem that's blocking your understanding, do you think?

Rae: I mean it's explained further on.

[John goes on for a number of turns explaining a point of grammar that he notices]

John: I don't want to focus too much on grammar. . . .

Rae: Oh, I see.

John: Because if you're having trouble with the book, I want to focus more on that.

Rae: OK. That's fine.

John: Let me finish reading this. Did you finish this whole book or no?

Rae: I read the whole book, but really I just didn't have much of a feeling about what was going on and what it was about. . . . And things suddenly would change and go on to a different part of the story, and I tend to get really lost.

John: Is this nonfiction?

Rae: It's a true story.

John: OK. It might in some way have to do with you, with it being bland . . . I think that was the word you used?

Rae: Just to me it seemed really bland and boring.

John: Historical novels—

Rae: I did try to understand what this guy was going through, but I still don't have a good understanding of what he went through.

John: What about *The Underdogs?* How did that go for you? Did that work for you? Did you understand that? The other novel, or the other book, rather?

Rae: Well, that *is The Underdogs.*

John: Oh, OK, yeah, you're right. Excuse me. OK. How about *Castro and Cuba?*

Rae: Yeah, that was better because there were *pictures* in the book, and this sort of thing. And . . . it tells me some historical

information that's clear . . . and not so roundabout. I feel like
sometimes I guess I'd rather find the point out about something
and how it becomes a part of our history.

John: OK, so maybe *The Underdogs* was not very direct. Is that it? Did
you kind of—

Rae: Right.

I reproduce this dialogue because it illustrates several important points.
Deaf culture values directness, which, as mentioned earlier, Rae confirmed in an interview. Later she also said that she was a visual learner
and thus preferred books with pictures, which helped her mentally
visualize the information. Rae preferred texts that are direct, express
emotion, and have this visual quality. When doing research and printing
things from the Internet in subsequent tutoring sessions, she admitted
that if the material was extremely long (and text heavy), she would not
read it.

In the last two tutoring sessions I observed with Blue and Newby,
they worked on reading for two different projects. Newby sees the value
of reading. She always encouraged Blue to read, recommended books
to her, and, at the last tutoring session I observed, presented Blue with
a book as a gift. Blue wanted to read more and develop her vocabulary
and comprehension skills. She also wanted to work on grammar in her
writing, and the tutoring sessions that I observed with Blue focused on
revising for LOCs and on reading.

Because she was concerned about failing science, Blue scheduled a
meeting with her science teacher. The teacher told her not to worry
but asked her to summarize the material in her book for a quiz, so she
brought her science book to the tutoring session with Newby. She had
read part of a chapter but did not understand it. Newby began by asking
Blue whether she understood the title of the chapter, then guided her
through some questions and answers and encouraged Blue to write the
concepts in her own words. The notion of putting something in one's
own words is both interesting and problematic for a deaf student using
an interpreter because sometimes the words are not the student's but the
interpreter's. At one point Newby began reading aloud with Jay interpreting, and then Newby said, "I think I want her to read this as opposed

to you signing it and my reading it. OK?" They spent the rest of the session with Blue reading bits of text, putting them into her own words, negotiating the meaning, and then writing it down. This process was extremely tedious, so not much ground was covered.

In the next session, they worked on paraphrasing a printout from the Internet. Here is part of the exchange to illustrate both the process and the interpretation issues:

Newby:	OK. And in addition to passion, what else do you need? Read this sentence again [pointing to paper].
Blue:	[goes to write]
Newby:	What is that? You tell me first.
Blue:	I don't know what "desire" means.
Newby:	OK. Desire. [to Jay] Are you telling her? OK.
Jay [interpreter]:	I was just showing her the sign for it.
Blue:	It's like—
Jay:	Spell what you just said.
Blue:	It means you're . . . eager.
Jay:	The interpretation is really wack right now, but come on.
Blue:	You need to want it.
Newby:	There you go. That's a very good word. You said "eager." You're eager for something, or you want it really badly. Yes.
Blue:	And should I just put down "and"?
Newby:	You have to write it in a sentence [pointing to paper]. "And you have to want it very badly, you have to really, really want it."
Jay:	I'm sorry, I'm trying to get her to give me the word, not the word I just gave her. That would be my interpretation of the word.
Newby:	You don't have to say "so badly" because you said "really badly." Take off "so badly." "Really, really want it." You could put "very badly" [pointing to paper]. Take out "so" and put "very."
Blue:	[writing]

They used the same pattern they had used in the previous session: Blue would read, then put the text into her own words, negotiate the meaning, and then write it down. It is clear from the preceding dialogue how the interpretation becomes an issue in paraphrasing and summarizing printed material.

Kali briefly worked on reading with Gustav when she was not sure of her interpretation of a poem she was explicating. Kali opened her book and showed Gustav the stanza she was unsure about: "Yes, the first two lines of the last stanza. . . . I wasn't really sure of the interpretation of that part." Gustav asked Kali what she felt the stanza meant and then assured her that she had already covered her interpretation of this portion of the stanza in her explication:

> I think, then, if that's your interpretation . . . of that part of the poem,
> I think you explain it well enough when you talk about [the fact]
> that she is on the road to heaven just by being herself and remaining
> a good person. I would say that you're covering that as a matter of
> interpretation.

Kali reported that she enjoyed reading and had read a lot as a child. She also mentioned that she got most of her information from reading. This is clear by what she worked on—explication of poetry is a higher level of reading than simple reading for information.

Squirt was the only hearing student to work on reading, probably because she was the only one who was taking a literature class. While revising her paper on *Giovanni's Room,* her tutor, Newby, encouraged her to add more examples from the text to strengthen her assertions. They spent a lot of time reading through the book, finding certain passages and examples. At times they read pertinent sections aloud. They also looked for page numbers for citations and talked about paraphrasing. Newby asked Squirt clarifying questions about what she had written, and Squirt attempted to answer by finding material in the book to illustrate her points:

> Newby: [Did David have anything to do] with Giovanni's death?
> Squirt: I don't think—I don't remember what happened. Do you
>   know what chapter it happened [in]?

Newby: No.
Squirt: [looks in book] Come on, where's the stinkin' chapter? Oh,
         yeah.

The focus of the reading with Squirt and Newby was not understanding
the text but finding instances in the text to back up Squirt's argument.

Research

Rae, Kali, and Herrodrick worked on or talked about research in their
tutorials. Rae was the only tutee to actually do research during a session.
She asked John to help her study for a Spanish history final, for which
she needed to define a number of terms. In two of the three tutorials
I observed between Rae and John, they decided to search the Internet
rather than look through Rae's notes. One or the other or both would
look for the term she needed and then print out the material they had
found. These were not tutorials in writing per se, but Rae and John had
a standing appointment at the writing center and would work on whatever topics Rae wanted.

  This Internet research resulted in two minor controversies. The first
was that Rae's teacher had told her not to use the Internet to study for
the test, but John and Rae did so anyway. The other was that the printouts used up immense amounts of paper. This was problematic for Rae in
two ways. First, as an environmentalist, she was concerned about wasting
paper, and because of the length of the printouts, she said she probably
would not read them: "It's just too long. I'm just going to throw it away
and not even read it. If it was a page I might read it." These sessions could
be seen as anomalies, but I myself have had sessions as a writing center
tutor where the tutee and I went to the computer to do some research
relevant to the student's paper, either on the Internet or in a database. So,
I believe doing actual research in the tutorial is a relevant activity even
though I found only one tutee in the study who did so.

  Kali and Gustav discussed research in relation to her Ray Bradbury
paper. Kali mentioned that she had to include criticism, and Gustav recommended that she consult with the reference librarian about the multivolume
works on short-story criticism that could be found in the reference section.

Herrodrick and John also discussed research in relation to Herrodrick's paper on a Trix commercial. John asked Herrodrick whether he could somehow get a copy of the TV commercial to view. Herrodrick said that he could get one at a television broadcast museum nearby. Herrodrick had clearly prepared for this research: "They said they have . . . archives on the second floor." In the end, however, Herrodrick happened to see the commercial on TV, so he did not have to go to the museum after all.

Relationship of Reading to Lower-Order Concerns

The focus of tutoring sessions between deaf tutees and hearing tutors seems to be quite similar to those between hearing tutees and hearing tutors, but there are some differences. The most obvious ones are reading and attention to lower-order concerns. It is not surprising that all of the deaf tutees had tutoring sessions that focused on LOCs and reading. Throughout the literature on deafness, these two themes are highlighted as important.

Because all of the deaf tutees in the study needed help with reading and because reading is typically difficult for deaf people (Paul 1998), most deaf tutees will likely need some help with this literacy skill. This statement is reinforced by my experiences with one deaf and one hard of hearing tutee I observed (not included in the final data set), who needed such assistance. In fact, for some deaf students, difficulty in reading English is a real barrier to learning. Some researchers (e.g., Johnson 1996) blame this problem on cultural factors and a lack of schema. Others (e.g., Paul 1998) maintain that, for some deaf students, insistence on text-based literacy may even be oppressive. Deaf students have varying levels of reading ability (Schmitz 2008), and not all deaf students will have problems with reading. However, it is reasonable to expect that deaf students are more likely to need help with reading than their hearing counterparts.

Written text can also be seen as adequate input in English for deaf students (Johnson 1996; Supalla 1986), meaning that English input is fully accessible to deaf people only through text, but their lack of schema and vocabulary may prevent some deaf students from acquiring English in this way. Another problem is that deaf students read mostly for semantic meaning, not syntactic meaning. Complex syntactic structures can be challenging for some deaf students (Kelly 1987; Richard Nowell, pers. comm.). Revising for LOCs relates to deaf students' struggles with surface features of English, sometimes referred to as "deafisms," which are supposedly typical mistakes or errors that deaf writers make, but the earlier discussion shows that both deaf and hearing students generally work on the same or similar surface concerns. The difference appears to be that deaf students work more on grammar—things like verb tense and article use—than hearing students, who are familiar with standard English. In addition, speakers of nonstandard dialects, like Shareef (or maybe it would be better to say students unfamiliar with print conventions), also need to work on grammar. Writing center practitioners may be reinforcing this weakness through read-aloud proofreading techniques. Shareef, the only hearing speaker of a nonstandard dialect in the study, reports that reading aloud does him no good in helping him to find his errors because, when he reads, it sounds fine, but he can see his errors when he looks at them on the page.

All of the participants in the study, both deaf and hearing, engaged in revision for LOCs, but different tutees did so to different extents, and revising for LOCs appears to be another key category for deaf students. Most of the tutoring dyads and triads in the study did not focus exclusively on LOCs but dealt with them briefly as they came up. Blue and Shareef, however, focused on them in similar fashion. Both of their tutoring sessions concentrated primarily on LOCs. This is interesting, as Blue is deaf and Shareef is hearing, and they had different tutors. What they have in common is that they are both African American and working class and come from the inner city. While I cannot make a specific connection, it is interesting that the two black students in the study spent most of their tutoring time doing line-by-line error correction.

I discussed this observation and the possibility of differential treatment with their tutors. Newby feels she needs to work with the students where they are and where they feel comfortable, and for many inner-city students, acquiring standard American English and writing correct prose are their first goals: "The language issue is a real issue when it comes to standard English on paper." Once students become comfortable with the written code, they can move on to other matters. Newby feels that inner-city and working-class students feel uncomfortable with the standard forms and therefore want to work on them. She feels that tutors would perhaps be doing them a disservice by ignoring these issues.

John, who tutored Rae, Herrodrick, and Shareef, feels that not working on surface features with students who struggle with standard English is a disservice to them since teachers grade them on these forms: "Most teachers are looking at surface form, and I think that it's probably my job to help with that more so than help with other things." John also believes that race and class are a factor only if they have influenced a student's educational preparation. I surmised that the difference is urban/suburban, but tutor Gustav told me he had received a very good education at a very bad suburban school; however, this still reinforces the urban/suburban split.

Lately, when discussing this issue with colleagues, someone brought up the argument that student achievement, and hence preparation, is in direct relation to the amount of money spent on children in the school system, and research bears this out (Condron and Roscigno 2003). Irrespective of student background and educational preparation, I believe the differences relate directly to reading and familiarity with printed materials. Students who read less are going to be less familiar with print conventions and will need more work on mastering them. Deaf participant Kali, for instance, is a big reader and does not have the problems with surface forms and reading comprehension that Blue (who does not read much) has even though they are both deaf women and members of ethnic minorities.

Perhaps trouble with reading and with surface features are related, as Johnson (1996) states that deaf students' literacy problems stem not from their deafness but from inadequate input, especially in the form of written English. Or perhaps deaf students' unfamiliarity with print conventions causes them not to notice their mechanical and grammatical errors (Hartwell 1980). Another possibility is that deaf students are going through a normal second-language acquisition sequence (Dulay, Burt, and Krashen 1982). My own idea is that inadequate input during the critical period and beyond may cause deaf learners to form an internal language structure that resembles a pidgin or creole more than a full grammar of English *or* ASL. While this is a compelling idea, I do not develop it here but rather leave the question open for those with more training in psycholinguistics to answer. Yet another likelihood is that students who are signing in PSE believe that what they are signing is English; thus, they think that if they put down on paper exactly what they are signing (excluding crucial nonmanual elements like eye gaze and facial expression), they are writing English (Mashie 1995).

INTERLUDE

———

Tutors

John

John had been a tutor at Davis College for two years when we started our observations. John, who is a white hearing male in his early twenties, is a film major. He took the tutor-training course at Davis with the writing center director, Ann, and found it to be valuable. In addition, he said that how he tutors is instinctual and that through his experiences, it is subjective. The course readings did not necessarily influence him, but without the course he would not be able to tutor as well as he does. Even though he found the course indispensable, when he is in a tutoring session, his instincts kick in.

When I asked Brock, the assistant director, why he had chosen John to work with Rae, he replied that many factors influence the pairing up of tutor and deaf student:

> In the case of Rae this year, I was looking at the schedule, and I noticed she expressed a desire to work with someone in film. And my goal was to hopefully get her with an instructor—one of the instructors we have here who teaches film as well. And I was able to get her with him for one hour, and then the other hour I put her

with John, a film student. . . . What I've observed with John, sitting
in on his sessions, is that . . . he's extremely concerned with . . . doing
the best for the student . . . he's always got a stack of handbooks, and
he's ready to go. There's a sense that . . . he's there for them. . . . I let
him know ahead of time that I placed her with him and, if he felt that
that was more than he was able to handle, let me know, but he, being
John, and not surprisingly, said, "No, that's fine." . . . And actually, in
this case, what had happened is that Rae actually felt more comfortable to work with John and asked to switch her hour with . . . the
instructor to John, so, I mean, it is nice.

While watching the sessions and talking to John, I noticed that he takes
pains to be thorough and precise and to ensure that the students understand
the material, both course content and grammatical information. He noted
that, in his tutoring sessions, "The main objective is to really be specific and
thorough. Because it's just one on one. There aren't thirty students. So you
can just focus in on one particular thing that needs to be focused on or
one particular subject or whatever. . . . It's extremely important in tutoring
sessions to be thorough." His goals for the sessions are for the student to
acquire "a better understanding of . . . what they need to know . . . to come
out of here knowing something better than they did before." He indicated
that he worked with several students, both deaf and hearing, on "concepts."
  John is careful to give explanations when he tutors. He said, "You
don't just want to tell them, 'Do this, do that' . . . you need to be thorough
and explain to them . . . an explanation is always required." John does not
like to concentrate on grammar: "I try to focus on the content of their
work. . . . Grammar is usually the last thing I focus on." In addition, he
realizes that not all of the students are going to be interested and engaged:
"There's some students who are going to show up every week, and some
students who won't, and some students aren't gonna care." About his
tutoring technique, he said, "I don't want to tell them if the content
of their paper is correct or incorrect. In terms of grammar . . . I never
tell them that it is incorrect. I try to give them explanations and show
them. I refer to *A Writer's Reference*. . . . [But] if they don't wanna learn,
then they don't wanna learn. I try my best." I confirmed these observations through my conversations with Brock and by watching John tutor.

Several times he referred the students to the handbook and explained to them they could look up the rules there and do some exercises to learn more. He believes that "the fundamentals of writing: that's something that you could learn [on your own] or can be taught."

John is truly committed to student learning: "I have a different dynamic with every student, so you have to kind of structure each session differently, so you can work with the student best." He is also very flexible with the subject matter: "As long as I can help them, I'll tutor them in just about any subject. As long as it in one way or another concerns writing. All the tutors [here at Davis] are very inclusive when it comes to what they are willing to tutor." His general philosophy is to treat all of the students the same. With a deaf student he said it was important not to "treat her as a special case; don't treat her as an anomaly . . . just look at whatever needs that student has and try to accommodate that . . . your job is to help them, and, besides that, just try to approach it the same way every time."

Although at first he was nervous when he learned he would be working with a deaf student, he found that working with a deaf student is very much the same as working with a hearing student: "There's probably not that much of a difference . . . the only difference is it's not one on one; there's the interpreter." With the interpreter he finds that the communication is generally good: "It's almost like a one-on-one session in terms of communicating." The only changes he has to make have to do with timing, for instead of "a . . . conventional conversation [where] you . . . overlap them," with an interpreter present, "I wait for her to finish, and then there's more breaks and pauses." He also noted the importance of waiting if the student is doing something: "If she's not looking—let's say she's writing something—you're speaking to her, and she's writing this down, [and] then you want to say something else, you have to wait so she looks up, and she can gather herself and then look at the interpreter." John worked with only one deaf tutee, Rae, and in their sessions they worked a great deal on "conceptualizing things" and "understanding stuff" rather than editing and revising papers, as many hearing students want to do. Referring to Rae, he said, "Her needs are different, but the actual process of the session is the same." He found her to be "very interested" in her work, and he was glad to be able to help her.

Newby

Newby, a tutor at Davis College, also works with special needs students in the public schools. It was her second semester tutoring at Davis when I began my observations; previously she had taught special education in the public high schools and tutored for literacy volunteers. A middle-aged, hearing black woman, Newby is a reflective, caring tutor. In addition to the session log that the writing center requires, she keeps her own journal of all of her tutoring sessions. She was the only tutor in the study to do this. As an older tutor and a grandmother in real life, Newby reflected that she has a motherly or grandmotherly relationship with some of her tutees.

Newby had a career in the military before enrolling in a master's degree program in special education and eventually studying for her doctorate. She is a published scholar in education, although she is not currently making progress toward her dissertation. Since she has experience carrying out naturalistic research, she understood the technical aspects of the study quite well and even gave me advice about camera and microphone placement. When I mentioned to Newby the echoes of Plato I heard in her tutoring sessions, she said the theorist she was more influenced by was Bakhtin. She calls herself a radical constructionist. She was the only tutor in the study to explicitly call forth theory in relation to tutoring and teaching. She has not taken a formal tutoring course but has read all of the material required for tutors at Davis.

Newby's general philosophy of learning includes a belief in the importance of reading ("I'm totally convinced that reading will help you in your writing"), and she often worked with students on understanding what they read so they would be able to write about it. She has a keen interest in adolescent literature, especially Newberry award winners. She also worked on learning ASL during the time of our observations; she opined wistfully, "I wish I could sign." Newby mentioned that she tried to encourage students by telling them to "slow down, take your time; you can find your errors." She is very student-centered and believes "we need to . . . try to understand where the student is and how to proceed from there." Reflecting on being honest with her tutees about their weaknesses, she said, "You have to develop a rapport and kind of learn [to know] your students before you can say some things. Because sometimes there are things that I think I should say, but the time is not right. . . . Then I feel that I'm failing them in some way." She thinks it is important not only to accept what the students do but also to "develop the rapport to be able to tell them" things that are not always positive; in this way tutors and tutees can work together as equals.

Some of Newby's beliefs about tutoring include that "our first concern in tutoring should be global and understanding what's required." She believes that first she must "figure out where the student is and how the student will best accept help." She explained, "I've found that I try to work with the student where they are. . . . I usually ask a student in the beginning, 'How do you feel I can best help you?' " In tutoring, she feels that "you use whatever you have to connect with the student and make them understand." Newby added, "I tutor different students differently because we have students come with different ideas or perceptions and different attitudes." Sometimes she has resistant students, and she made it clear that her goal was to help them with their goals, and "often you have to bring the student around to wanting to do that." That understanding is important, and many times it is "going to improve his or her writing."

About tutoring deaf students in particular, Newby believes that "to them the most important thing is grammar because that's what they struggle with most." She also encouraged her deaf tutee, Blue, to get involved with Deaf culture, especially theater, since Blue wanted to be an actress. Specific techniques she uses with a deaf student are to have the interpreter transliterate what the student wrote and to attempt to focus the student's attention on the paper or the interpreter or wherever it needs to be. With a deaf student she focuses more on grammar, such as explicitly teaching about verbs, and on getting the student involved. When I asked whether any of these techniques went against her training, she replied, "Oh, yes. Oftentimes I will make more of the corrections than I should." She also noted that not all of the interpreters were as skilled and as thorough as her current interpreter, Linda.

About students with learning disabilities, she noted, "We pretty much work with [these] students the same way as we work with any student: as an individual. . . . [We are] helping the students to develop strategies that will aid them in their writing, and that's what you do with all the students." Newby was working on a workshop about students with learning disabilities in the semester when I made my observations, and she had previously presented on the topic at a national conference. Her work with these students showed her that many of them "don't have a linear learning style; they're global or spatial. And they have trouble expressing in the linear fashion that's required to succeed in education." She explained that "working with 'special ed' really impacts how I work with students because you realize that you have to teach the [individual] student—meet the students where they are . . . the fact that that is my specialty has a big impact on how I tutor."

Gustav

Gustav is a white hearing man in his thirties. He has a master's degree in political science. He formerly taught political science at Stanhope College, tutored students in math and political science, and also taught at a school for people with cognitive disabilities. At the time of the study he had garnered three years of experience as a tutor. Gustav's tutor training consisted of workshops and breakout sessions and viewing the video series *The Tutor's Guide* (1986). When there was a need for English tutors, he switched, and now he tutors English one day a week. His full-time job is working in a residence for adults with developmental disabilities, whom he is extremely comfortable working with. Gustav continues tutoring because he enjoys both the work and his colleagues: "We do have a pretty good group. Very, very friendly, very open to communication." He is also a published poet.

Gustav knows a little bit of sign language, but he does not use it in the tutoring sessions: "I do have some rudimentary knowledge of sign language. I don't let on that I do because I know just enough to sign the wrong things." He feels that "the only real difference between working with someone with a hearing disability and someone who does not have one is that there's a lack of confidentiality. There's one other person there. So perhaps the tutoring sessions are a bit more public . . . one of our ideals here is confidentiality between the tutor and the student." He should not have to feel this way since the interpreter's work is also confidential.

When tutoring a deaf student, Gustav tries "to treat everybody the same. When I'm working with someone who's deaf, I will look at them and not the interpreter. . . . I'm looking at them but hearing the interpreter, and pretty much the interactions are pretty similar." He feels that "it's better to work with deaf students in a more directive manner. But I've been trained in a nondirective, noninterventionist kind of tutoring where—hands off—you don't do anything, you just kind of sit there and let the student do everything. So, I'm still uncomfortable with that even though I know it's the right way to do it." Gustav has a lot of experience working with people with disabilities, but he wants to learn more: "What's most important for me is to have more exposure to different people with different disabilities, with different language, different modes of communication."

Some tutoring techniques Gustav uses with hearing students are reading their papers aloud "so the student can hear the paper and hear how the paper flows. So the student might be able to stop you and say, 'It's not what I meant,' or . . . something that's more obvious to the student when the student's hearing it . . . instead of just looking at it." Occasionally he also reads the paper silently and marks the things he wants to talk about. He feels very strongly about the interpersonal dimension of the tutoring session:

> Relationships are very important to me. And so I try to pretty much have a conversation that benefits the student. I don't want it to be a cold business experience . . . If the student wants it to be very cold and impersonal . . . that's fine. But I like the relational aspect of it. I will often see students several semesters after I'm done working with them. And that's very pleasant to me. So, I would say that's my philosophy on it.

Another technique Gustav sometimes uses with lower-level students is to explain a rule, but with most students he just suggests that they go look it up on their own time. His most important philosophy is that "people have diverse needs." Although he attempts to be flexible in the tutoring sessions, sometimes he feels this attitude has more to do with his mood or his energy level:

> I might be tired, or . . . [I might not] have the mental energy to do justice to the "hands off" [technique.] . . . If I'm very tired, I might have the tendency to wanna make the time count for something and also to address the problems as quickly and as clearly as I can. Whereas if I have a bit more energy, feel a little better, I might . . .

put the student in the direction and watch her develop . . . perhaps depending on my mood or how I feel, I might move in the direction of student motivation, watch the student do everything and [assume either] a very passive role or a more active role.

About tutoring in general, Gustav sometimes experiences "a certain level of anxiety" about the tutoring session, and "there's always a desire . . . to do well by the student." He believes that a successful tutoring session is "one in which the student greatly benefits and learns something new." It is important for him that "the student is completely in control . . . they will have an assignment which they are working on." But Gustav is careful not to give all of the control to the student if the student is on the wrong track: "It's important to us not to lead the student down the wrong path. If we're helping the student write a paper that's completely inappropriate to the assignment, it's going to be counterproductive."

CHAPTER 4

⟨———⟩

How Tutoring Gets Done

I don't think [tutoring is] the kind of thing I'm going to be able
to read in an article. I think I have to experience it.

—Gustav

Through my grounded-theory coding and analysis of the tutoring sessions, I found that the tutors and students engaged in two
primary kinds of interactions—*taking charge* and *making sense,* based on
either (1) discourse or interaction or (2) texts. Taking charge is the act of
control, which may or may not be conscious and deliberate. Participants
controlled (or attempted to control) the flow of information and/or the
other person's behavior during conversation and text discussion. During
conversation, this manifests as information- and behavior-based discourse. The former refers to control of the give-and-take of information.
Tutors and tutees asked for, volunteered, or sometimes even withheld
information. The latter refers to attempting to direct or alter the other
participant's behavior, usually with the goal of improving the text.

Text-based acts of taking charge refer to control and use of print and
digital materials for a specific outcome. Making sense refers to understanding (or attempting to understand) the other person or the content
of the discussion. Making sense with discourse is the use of conversation to enhance understanding between the participants. Making sense

75

TABLE 5. *Tutoring Interactions*

	Taking Charge	Making Sense
Discourse-Based		
Information	improving the paper	discussing ideas
	test questioning/nondirective tutoring	explaining/asking for an explanation
		confirming/understanding
		procedure/clarification questioning
Behavior	negotiating session focus	
	directing behavior	making sense of behavior
	monitoring	
Text Based	finding and correcting errors	reading
	taking charge of text	writing
		evaluation

with text refers to either producing or discussing texts with the goal of enhanced understanding (table 5).

Each of the tutoring sessions I observed had a natural flow, though the procedures varied according to the tutees' needs in a particular session. The following list outlines these procedures. The tutee came in with or without a paper.

— If the tutee had a finished paper, the dyad would either go over it for correctness or teacher comments, put it aside and begin the next task, or reflect on it.

— If the tutee had a paper in progress, the dyad would read it and discuss higher-order concerns, lower-order concerns, or both.

— If the tutee had no paper and no new paper assignment to work on, the session could be cancelled, as happened with Kali, or the dyad would work on something else, such as reading and research in Blue's and Rae's individual cases. Or, they would go over a previous paper, as in the case with Blue's Janet Jackson paper.

— If the tutee had no paper but had an assignment, the dyad would discuss ideas for it. If the paper was finished but the tutee did not bring it, the dyad would discuss the ideas in it.

Knowing the general flow of the tutoring session should help the reader to follow this discussion more easily.

In this study, the terminology that relates to tutoring is controversial. The common term "talk" is based on a hearing reality, where people speak and listen. Margaret Weaver (1996) criticizes the term "conversation" when applied to deaf students as she feels it implies speech and hearing. I think it is appropriate here, however, because conversation can take place via talking or signing, an interpreter, and even text (e.g., instant messaging or other computer/text-based communication). Tutoring with a deaf student can also involve writing on paper, and that, too, is written conversation. In the following I use "discourse" and "conversation" rather than "talk" as generic labels that include both signed and spoken modalities of language.

Taking Charge

Taking charge is a phrase that John used in our interview of October 15, 2003, and it worked perfectly as an *in vivo* code for the concept of control. John was talking about Rae, who tended to take charge in their sessions, unlike the other tutees, who appeared to allow the tutor to control the discussion most of the time. Session participants took charge of and through discourse or text. In the following sections I discuss tutors and tutees grouped by relevance to the topic under discussion. Those who did not engage in one interaction or another are skipped in that section.

Discourse-Based Taking Charge

Discourse-based taking charge involves the control or elicitation of information or behavior through conversation. Both tutors and tutees attempted to meet their goals for the session by asking for information and negotiating behavior. This is an important category of analysis because participants in the tutoring session worked together in order to achieve their objectives, which, in contrast to Stephen North's (1984a) axiom about making better writers, was usually an improved paper.

Taking Charge of Information

Taking charge of information includes imparting information, test questioning, and nondirective tutoring. Both tutors and tutees imparted information in the sessions, but tutors gave explicit advice and information in the form of insider knowledge of the conventions of writing and the teachers' expectations. Tutees usually imparted information about their assignment, topic, or writing process, usually in response to a tutor's question. Here I discuss taking charge of improving the tutee's paper.

Improving the Paper.   Occasionally the information was the tutor's idea of what the tutee should do with the paper. The tutors sometimes directly told the tutees what to do about their papers, which was clearly taking charge of information, especially if it was not in response to a tutee's question about what to do. For example, John gave explicit advice to Shareef about how to focus his paper:

> Just don't make the foundation of this paper be about performing. I mean, you could if you want to. If you wanna write about writing and about your skills as a writer, then make the foundation of the paper about writing. That should be the core of the paper. . . . If you want to make it performing, then you have to switch it all around and have that be the . . . foundation and have everything kind of revolve around that.

John was the only peer tutor in the study, yet his peer status did not stop him from explicitly taking charge of a tutee's paper. With Herrodrick, John couched most of his directives in conditional language, but it is clear that John had no problem giving direct advice on what to do with a paper, as this excerpt from one of his tutoring sessions with Herrodrick shows:

> And just talk primarily about what it is exactly in these ads. Or this ad, because you probably want to try to pick one, if you can find one, to try to make it more specific, really kind of break it down. What is it in that ad specifically that they're doing? So you can . . . keep the same

intro to a certain extent. Maybe omit a couple of things, like talking about how they brainwash and all that stuff. And then after you have a specific commercial, you can say, "And my example is so and so and so," and you can use the body of the paper to talk about that.

When tutoring Rae, John was also explicit: "You have to include this question also . . . on your paper: 'Why do people write history? Should history be a story?'"

In contrast, Gustav phrased most of his suggestions in a conditional way, as if he were writing the paper himself. For example, he said, "I wouldn't start this sentence with 'but.'" In some cases, however, he slipped into explicitly telling Kali how to organize and focus her paper, as in this series of comments:

> I actually want you to keep the sentence, but I want the focus of the paragraph to change, from *Fahrenheit 451* to the dangers of mass culture. So, I'd actually like to keep . . . this sentence.
> [a few turns later]
> OK. I would incorporate a couple more of those in either this paragraph or one additional paragraph. But solely on how they relate to mass culture. Nothing else. OK. And just keep the focus on mass culture. So, whatever you do with the rest of this paragraph here, try to fit it in somewhere else. Don't keep it—you don't have to throw it out, but don't keep it in the same paragraph.

Gustav used the conditional in the beginning of the second exchange, but it appears that he got carried away with the topic and the organizational scheme of Kali's paper and forgot to use the polite conditional. This is interesting because, in orthodox tutoring, tutors are not supposed to tell tutees what to do with their papers, but clearly in practice they do. The use of grammatical devices like the conditional mask the directiveness of the exchange, but it is still there. The tutor gave the tutee direction on how to improve the paper. It is worth remembering that the tutors in this study were chosen by their directors for their work with deaf students because they were trusted for their tutoring ability.

Newby is an adherent of nondirective tutoring, yet she, too, directed tutees on how to improve their papers on occasion. For instance, when tutoring Blue she said the following:

> You've got to write more to add to this. What you've done is good, but you need to add more. So, you didn't say that in here, so maybe you can say it now. You just kind of summarized everything up. But now, to lengthen this, you need to add more, so you're gonna kind of break it down and write more sentences.

And with Squirt she said the following:

> But you're gonna have to tell . . . something about that relationship. I also think you need to talk about—you mentioned David's struggle, but you've got to move in time from here to here. You can't just throw the sentences there.

So, she did give Squirt the "tips" she desired from time to time, although most of Newby's tutoring was nondirective.

Test Questioning and Nondirective Tutoring. Taking charge by questioning for information is a way to control the session. The tutor may not even be aware of this as a control factor, as asking questions has become a generally accepted way to tutor. It is actually better when the tutee asks the questions, as Squirt did quite often. When the tutors asked questions, it was not only for nondirective tutoring, although that is what immediately comes to mind. They also asked probing or expanding questions, looking for more information, as Newby did: "What about this? [Janet Jackson] recorded it in 1984, OK. What about this?" Johnson (1993) suggests that questions may not be as effective as is commonly thought. She explains that questions can actually shut down communication rather than open it up. In fact, statements can actually generate more response from a tutee than questions.

Nondirective tutoring works for many students but is not always successful with deaf students and those with learning disabilities. For instance, consider the following nondirective exchange between Newby and Blue:

Newby: "Norman Lear wanted her." There's a word left out here. "Wanted her."

Blue: Meaning Janet Jackson.

Newby: N–n–n–n–n–n–no.

Blue: I took it from something else, and I made some changes. Really, the paper said "offered her" but kind of "ordered her," so I made some changes. My own words.

Newby: That's OK. You just left out a word. You just left out a word. This is the kind of thing you have to work on putting it on paper. When you're signing it, maybe some prepositions drop or helping verbs or whatever, but when you're putting it on paper, remember when we put it on paper everything needs to be . . . So you've just gotta . . . What word would you put in here? [pointing to paper]

Blue: In?

Newby: "In" would be good, but I don't think it's what you're trying to say. I mean, "in" would work, but I don't think that's what you were trying to say. "He wanted her blank a job."

Blue: Work?

Newby: Well, you could say he wanted her to work, but if you put one word here [pointing to paper], "wanted her" . . .

Blue: To?

Newby: You could say "to do," but, but [five-second pause, Newby is thinking] . . . OK now [four-second pause while looking at paper], "wanted her for a job." Make sense? Does that make sense to you?

Blue: Yeah.

There is only one question here, "What word would you put here?" But it is a question to which the tutor knows the answer. It appears that the tutor was working with a conception of an ideal text. Rather than accept the words Blue offered, which could have been made to work in the sentence, the tutor continued until it was clear that Blue was not going to offer the word Newby was looking for. After nine turns, Newby offered her own solution. She then asked whether Blue understood, which was a genuine question for sense making. In retrospect, it might have been more effective for Newby to abandon nondirective tutoring and provide the student with the word or attempt to use one of the words Blue offered.

Nondirective tutoring can also be frustrating for students with a learning disability, such as Squirt, a hearing student. Newby's nondirective questions clearly frustrate her, but they find a way to work it out in the end:

[they are discussing *Giovanni's Room*]
Newby: David, the story's about David, right? Was David a straight guy or a gay guy?
Squirt: We don't know.
Newby: Did David know?
Squirt: No.
Newby: Did he know in the end?
Squirt: I don't think so, no.
Newby: Why didn't he know?
Squirt: I don't know, you gotta read the story.
Newby: I don't have to read the story, I have to read your paper.
Squirt: I don't remember. Ask [the teacher]. She'll tell you. I don't know.
Newby: Come on, Squirt, let's stop that.
Squirt: I don't know. I told you, I don't remember. I read the story two months ago.
Newby: So what do you think you need to do in order to be able to write?
Squirt: I'm not reading it again.
Newby: So, what—Do you plan to pass the class?
Squirt: Yeah.
[They discuss the importance of this paper to her grade]
Newby: Because, I mean, what's, why, why is this story so hard to write about?
Squirt: I don't know.

Newby: You've written about stories before.

Squirt: I don't know. It's just weird. I don't know, I don't know. I just wanna get this done and over with.

Newby: And do you wanna do a good job?

Squirt: If I get a C, that's fine.

Newby: Well, I mean, at this point, I don't even think you've got a C.

Squirt: It's a D paper? I don't know. Well, then, that's why you're supposed to help me.

Newby: I'm trying to help you, Squirt. What would you have me do?

Squirt: I don't know, just read it and let me know what you think or something.

Newby: I'm, I'm trying—

Squirt: You're not telling me, though.

Newby: I'm trying to get you to work through what you need to do to write this paper.

Squirt: OK.

Newby: It's your job to write the paper, not mine.

Squirt: I know. So what am I gonna do?

Newby: OK. You're gonna tell me about David, right? And you don't know if David was gay or straight?

Squirt: Right.

Newby: OK.

This rather long exchange illustrates the potential pitfalls of the nondirective technique for deaf students and students with a learning disability. Squirt quite clearly wanted Newby to give her a genuine response as a reader, to tell her things ("You're not telling me"), not just to ask questions. But earlier in the exchange, Newby had indicated that it had been thirty-four years since she had read the book, and she truly did not know the answers to these questions. At the same time she was probing for information in order to help Squirt understand how she needed to expand and develop her paper.

In her interview with me, Squirt said she wished Newby would "give more tips." The preceding exchange turned around when Newby began asking genuine questions for information like, "What would you have me do?" In terms of effectual and ineffectual tutoring practices, questions have their place, especially when they are genuine requests for information. Squirt turned the session around when she asked her own question: "So what am I gonna do?" Throughout her tutoring sessions, Squirt asked these kinds of operational, procedural questions, which she knew Newby could answer: "Do you want me to take it out?" "Well, then, how can I make it clear?" "So, how should I change it?" and "So, how should I analyze it?" Squirt also asked smart-alecky questions (discussed later; see *relating*).

Other tutees asked the same kind of direct questions as Squirt did. For instance, Kali asked Gustav questions like, "So, omit the 'a,' do you think?" "So, should I put down that that means the moon?" and "Where should this belong, this word that you wrote on?" In these examples the tutee takes charge by eliciting advice from the tutor, just the type of questioning that Johnson (1993) advocates. Blue also asked the tutor advice questions about what she should do: " 'And'—should I just put down 'and'?" Rae asked John, "What should I write?" Herrodrick asked John, "How would I go about that, though? Would I just omit it and replace it with a different word?" Shareef asked John, "I need a quotation mark?" These types of questions show the tutee taking charge by asking for direct answers from the tutor.

Questions can also be ineffectual, especially with a deaf student, when they are irrelevant curiosities of the tutor and a waste of the student's time. In an interview, Rae told me about a faculty tutor she had once had:

> I had another tutor. This guy was, I'm not gonna say his name, but this man was like, "What do you mean you don't understand English?" and "How can I help you change your English to ASL?" and it was like he was asking me these ridiculous questions. And . . . I wanted to tell him, the point of this tutoring session is for you to help me with my paper, not to ask me a lot of questions about my language choices. It was my language, period. I am supposed to be asking you to help me with the English language, not you asking me questions . . . in this short hour that we have together. And . . . he's like, "I want to know how I can help you understand English." And I thought, my gosh, you are just talking, and you are just going to talk through the interpreter, and the interpreter is gonna give me the information in

ASL, and then I'll—maybe have some cognitive understanding of how the English needs to be written for the paper. I mean, it was just such a waste of time. . . . he had no idea . . . [that] all he needed to do was just be patient with me and find out what I needed. And really, that's what John is doing, and that's really what I want.

Rae's problem is not unique. According to a recent conversation on a disabilities listserv that I subscribe to, it seems that women with disabilities are often confronted by people who ask intrusive questions about their disability. Tutors should be both aware of this and careful not to let too much curiosity cause them to cross boundaries of politeness and respect.

Reflections on Directiveness

The concepts of directiveness and nondirectiveness are still hotly contested in the writing center literature. Shamoon and Burns (1995) make an excellent case for directive tutoring. Students cannot be expected to know what they do not know. Nondirective tutoring cannot work for MLA style, for instance, or for conventions of the organization and layout of a paper. Especially for deaf students, who may lack schema and familiarity with print, the tutor would be remiss in not pointing out the best way to lay out a sentence or a paragraph. It is clear from the observations for this study that good tutors use directiveness with both deaf and hearing tutees. Clearly the hands-off or minimalist technique in tutoring needs to be rethought. I consider these tutors as informants of the expectations of academic discourse and culture for their tutees. Of course, tutees want tips on how to improve their papers, and it is all right for tutors to give them. Anything else would be unfair. If tutors have the necessary knowledge, they should share it (Grimm 1999).

Since Deaf culture values directness, there is a potential for miscommunication when a request is phrased as a polite question (in hearing culture). Some cultures use directness to achieve a behavioral result, but other cultures, such as mainstream American academia, use an indirect politeness formula (Michaels 1986; Delpit 1988; Ballenger 1992; Kutz 1997; Heath 1983). These structures and expectations can conflict, especially with deaf people, who value directness and may not understand the pragmatic function of an indirect request (Mindess 1999; Jay, interpreter).

However, the tutors in this study were directive in matters of form only, especially organization and mechanics. They maintained the writing center orthodoxy of not taking over the content of the writing and not adding their own materials and opinions. In contrast, John was very collaborative in his brainstorming session with Herrodrick, and he did add his own ideas to Herrodrick's, but since it was a collaborative effort, his offerings were appropriate. Tutor-training manuals should reflect this reality of tutoring, not an idealized notion, but I think the writing center community is beginning to accept that the nondirective way is not the only right approach. Carino (2003) values flexibility, as do Gillespie and Lerner (2003). "[T]o engineer peer tutoring techniques that divest the tutor of power and authority is at times foolish and can even be unethical" (Carino 2003, 98). Carino goes on to say that many writing centers "have the good sense to place student needs before orthodoxy" (2003, 112). The students in this study needed a certain amount of directive help, and for the most part they got it, although it was a struggle for Squirt, who wanted more directive help than she got from Newby:

> Squirt: I just don't want to do it.
> Newby: Then why did you come?
> Squirt: I don't know, to have you do it.
> Newby: Well, you know that's not about to happen. You know I can't do it for you.

At least Squirt is clear and direct about what *she* wants from the tutor. Of course, seasoned tutors like Newby can determine how much help is too much. In the end, however, all of the tutors in the study explicitly informed their tutees, both hearing and deaf, of ways to improve their papers.

Tutors should be aware of how students best process information and offer them help in doing so. It is also appropriate, as Newby did with Blue, to encourage the tutee to explore other ways to access information or to strengthen weak areas. Still, the tutors must respect the students' abilities and realize that every student is different. Some process information according to their preferences, and some, such as deaf students and students with learning disabilities, process information consistent with differences in hard wiring. I believe strongly in Gillespie and Lerner's (2003) philosophy that tutors must be able to *control* a wide variety of tutoring practices and have the *flexibility* to know when to use them and when to abandon them and try something else.

Taking Charge of Behavior

Tutors and tutees both took charge of behavior in the sessions. In contrast to taking charge of information, which is eliciting or asking for facts or ideas for composing or revising, taking charge of behavior involves attempting to influence the procedure or focus of the session to achieve one's goals through negotiation of session focus, directing behavior, and monitoring, which for the purpose of this study is upholding the teachers' expectations.

Negotiation of Session Focus.   The sessions I observed were different from the "unmarked" tutorial, where the participants are meeting for the first time and must get to know each other and the assignment before tutoring can begin. All of the tutoring dyads I observed were weekly appointments, and since I did not observe the first meetings of the semester, all of the dyads had already established a working relationship before I came to observe. For this reason, sometimes there was no negotiation of the session focus. It was tacit: in some cases the participants got right down to work, and in others it was very much implied that if there was an assignment or a draft, that is what they would work on. Rae, however, really did take charge in the way an ideal tutee is expected to, as described in the tutoring manuals—and it was John's reference to this behavior in an interview that inspired me to create and name the category. To illustrate, in the first tutorial I observed she said the following to John:

> So, what I'd like you to do is just to check out my paper, just to . . . make sure it makes sense. . . . I do have a lot more to go, but I'd like to get your feedback about . . . what more information I should add to it.

Rae is explicit about what she wants the tutor to do. In the second tutorial I observed, she was also direct with what she wanted from John: "Do you think it's possible to help me with my study skills?" In the third session she was not forthcoming with a plan, so John asked her, "So, how could we spend this time helping you study? What do you think the best approach is?" This tack gave control of the session back to Rae. John told me that he appreciated it when a tutee took charge and had some idea of what the session should accomplish. Otherwise, he ended up looking over the work and focusing on "deficiency."

I observed five tutoring sessions in all with Blue and Newby. The first one was the last tutoring session for the spring semester of 2003. Blue had finished all of her classwork for the semester, and Newby tried to get her to write reflectively about their tutoring sessions together. Blue seemed to be resisting, but later in an interview she told me that she had not understood that Newby wanted her to write. Since she appeared as if she did not want to write, Newby suggested that she get out a copy of a finished paper so they could go over it, which they did.

In the second tutoring session I observed, the next semester, Newby asked Blue, "What have we got for today?" Blue described her assignment and repeated her teacher's counsel to watch her tenses. Newby picked up on that and continued to go through the paper and the teacher's comments, helping Blue with verb tenses. The next tutoring session's negotiation of focus was similar. Newby asked Blue what she was working on, and Blue told her the teacher's intentions through Jay, the interpreter ("He wants me to correct some stuff"), and after discussing the teacher's comments on the paper, Newby asked, "So you want to go over this right now?" This negotiation seemed very collaborative, with neither one taking charge but rather a true negotiation. In the session of November 19, 2003, Newby began by asking Blue how about her meeting with her science teacher. Blue told her that it was all right, that she was not failing the class, and then Newby made a just assumption when she asked, "Is that [pointing to the science book] what we're gonna work on today?" Blue replied that she had to summarize a chapter in the book and asked whether they could work on that. In the last session I observed with Blue and Newby, after exchanges of teasing and of gift giving, Newby reached for Blue's paper and said, "Let's see what you have here today." This tacit negotiation of focus is as follows: if there is a paper, we will read it.

Kali and Gustav's sessions also revealed a tacit agreement that, if there was a paper, it would be read and commented on. Similar to the other dyads I observed, it was the tutor who commented on the paper. Gustav asked Kali whether she minded if he wrote on the paper, but the assumption appeared to be that they would read over papers in progress for HOCs and LOCs, so the task did not need to be negotiated. In the second session I observed with Kali and Gustav, Kali took charge of the session focus when she said, "I brought my poetry interpretation. [shows it to Gustav] . . . I wanted you to read over it and see if there was anything that I might be missing, or anything that I should add." When Gustav finished reading and commenting on it, Kali asked whether she had properly interpreted the last stanza. Gustav assured her that she had. In their last session together in the study, Kali also verbalized her goals for the session:

> I wanted you to read this over and give me your opinion. . . . I didn't write down enough things, you know. I didn't put all my thoughts together as I was writing my rough draft. And it seems like there's so much information, and I don't know how to put everything down on paper. So, read it and see what you think.

Kali clearly took charge of the goals for her sessions, and they are information based, not correctness based. Kali, like Rae, is an "ideal" tutee in this way.

Squirt's tutorials evinced no discussion of what she and Newby would work on. In both sessions I observed they just jumped right into her draft. With Shareef and John, the assumption also appeared to be that they would look at drafts. The only negotiation was which draft they would look at, what the assignment was, and what stage the draft was in at the moment. The beginning of the tape of the first session with Herrodrick and John was cut off. For the other two sessions, the focus of the first one was implied by John:

John: So, you've got your new assignment.
Herrodrick: Yeah.
John: What's the new assignment?

It is clear that they had a tacit, ongoing agreement that if Herrodrick had an assignment, they would work on it. For their last tutoring session together, Herrodrick had already turned in his final English paper, but he still had one more required tutoring session left. Herrodrick wanted to discuss his own writing, but John invoked the authority of the teacher, Brock, who is also the assistant director of the writing center, and suggested that they work on classwork that day and personal writing the next week. Since Herrodrick had not brought a copy of his finished paper, they simply discussed the ideas he had written about.

Tutors and tutees can negotiate the session focus in four ways: (1) the tacit way, where there is no discussion and the participants just jump right in, (2) the tutor asks what the tutee wants to work on, (3) the tutor suggests what they should work on, and (4) the tutee explicitly identifies something to work on. Each tutor and tutee in my observations had a different style. Rae and Kali took charge and explained what they wanted to do or waited for a tutor's question and answered it. Squirt and Shareef appeared to assume the content of the session would be their drafts. Herrodrick and Blue waited for the tutor to ask what they wanted to work on.

There was no clear pattern among the tutors. Sometimes they waited for the tutee to indicate an area or a project to work on, and if it was not forthcoming, they asked. I say this because some of the tutors' "What do you want to work on?" questions came on the second page of the transcript. Perhaps the ongoing nature of the standing tutorial appointment lends itself to a tacit agreement of session focus. The only clear pattern is that two of the deaf tutees (Kali and Rae) explicitly stated what they wanted from the session, but none of the hearing tutees did so. Perhaps this is related to the value the Deaf culture places on direct communication.

Since Rae and Kali were the only tutees in the study who made their plans and desires for the tutoring session explicit, perhaps this reflects Deaf people's value of straight talk. In this case, Deaf students' cultural patterns result in ideal tutee behavior, as many tutor-training books expect the writer to set the agenda (Capossela 1998; Meyer and Smith 1987; Ryan 2002). However, in other tutorials I observed there was a tacit agenda of "if there is a paper, we will work on it," which is the type of (non)agenda setting that Gillespie and Lerner (2003) discuss. Concern with making sense is perhaps a reflection of the importance of clear and easy communication to the Deaf community (Gannon 1981; Mindess 1999). Deaf tutees, like ESL students, are more likely to ask for explanation of points of grammar. Blue seemed to be satisfied with work on mechanics, as she told me in an interview that grammar was the main point she wanted to work on in her writing, in addition to vocabulary.

Directing Behavior.   Directing behavior is a way for participants to control the actions of their session partners. This involves instructing the session partner to engage in behaviors that will bring about the desired outcome for the session or the task at hand. Tutors and tutees used directing, pacing, focusing, guiding, suggesting, and questioning as ways to direct behavior in the session.

For instance, John directly told Shareef, "When you go back to *A Writer's Reference,* look this up, OK?" and "Read that back." John did not direct Herrodrick's behavior; he only gave suggestions on how to improve his paper. For instance, John said, "So, the number-one thing you want to do is pick something that you are passionate about." The strongest he got with Herrodrick was still very collaborative: "Let's pretend right now that we're gonna work with that just so we can talk about it." This was more of a guiding of the session. John also told Herrodrick, "Yeah, focus on that this weekend." In the last tutoring session I observed, Herrodrick had not brought his paper, but John still wanted to see it, so John said, "If you can remember, get a copy for me, and just drop it in my mailbox." This, of course, is directing behavior outside the tutoring session.

In one of Newby and Squirt's tutoring sessions, Newby directed Squirt's behavior when she said, "You cannot get frustrated and take this attitude of defiance," and "Just read this for me." Behavior can also be directed by a question:

Newby: Do you wanna read? [pushing the paper toward her]
Squirt: No, I don't wanna read. [pushing the paper back]

The tutee did not necessarily follow the tutor's wish. The exchange continues with Newby using logic to control Squirt's behavior:

Newby: If you start, for instance, we'll take turns. [pushing the paper back toward Squirt] If you read first, you'll have a smaller part.
Squirt: [begins reading]

Newby also used questions to direct Blue's behavior:

> Newby: So, do you have the page from the Internet that we used? Do
>   you have it with you?
> Blue: Yeah.
> Newby: Can you take it out please?

Newby also attempted to initiate an exchange like this with Squirt but was unsuccessful:

> Newby: Do you have the old [draft]?
> Squirt: No.
> Newby: Just this. OK.

If Squirt had had the paper, Newby might have followed the exchange as she did with Blue and asked Squirt to take out the paper. These questions can also be directives or suggestions for revision, as later in this same session Newby asked Squirt, "Can you kind of separate those [ideas] in some way?"

Not all of the dyads used questions to direct behavior. In the nine tutoring sessions I observed with John, he did not use this type of device at all. John just directly told the tutee what he wanted him to do. I also did not observe Gustav or Kali using this device to control behavior. At a few points in Kali's sessions, the interpreter or Kali asked for repetition, but this had to do with *communication,* not tutoring.

Sometimes tutors' attempts to direct the behavior of their deaf tutees were thwarted by cultural miscommunication. Newby wanted Blue to write, but instead of directing her, she used a polite form: "So . . . maybe you could write for me today." I learned from my interviews with Blue and reflection on them with Jay that, with deaf people, one must be direct to get the desired result. Perhaps if Newby had said, "I want you to write today," or "Please write for me today," she would have gotten a better result (Blue did not end up writing).

Tutees also directed or attempted to direct their tutor's behavior; for instance, Shareef told John, "Make a little note there on the side because that helps me, you know." Squirt told Newby, "Just keep on reading."

Herrodrick and John did not appear to direct each other's behavior except when John told Herrodrick to put the paper in his mailbox. The closest Herrodrick got to directing John's behavior was when he said, "Let me write this down." At the end of the first conference I observed with them, Herrodrick asked John, "Did you happen to read?" meaning the story or novel that he was working on. This could be understood as a tacit request for behavior because if John had not read it, the implication was that Herrodrick wished he would read it for the next time. So, this could be seen as a direct request for information or a subtle reminder for a certain behavior. Squirt directed Newby's behavior when she said in reference to Newby's understanding of her paper, "Don't forget you have to read it," meaning that she wanted Newby to finish reading her paper before starting to ask questions.

Rae and John were not shy about directing each other's behavior, especially when it came to the physical arrangement of their tutorial. For example, when John was typing at the keyboard, Rae told him to move so she could type. She also said, "You can tell me and I can type." Rae was the only tutee that took charge of the session in this way. She also attempted to control John's behavior by asking him, "Do you have a hole puncher that I could use?" and he replied, "Yeah, I think we have one up there. Do you want me to go get it?"

Kali directed Gustav's behavior only when she asked him to write a note for her, the way Shareef did: "Oh, let's put that down so that I don't forget it." She also gave him permission to write on her paper, which is not directing behavior but allowing it. Although she was explicit about what she wanted out of the session and often asked for repeats when she did not understand, she appeared much of the time to be a passive receptor of Gustav's comments, although she did back-channel from time to time.

Blue did not appear to direct Newby's behavior in the actual conference, but she did ask for a handout: "Yes, I need to write clear. Can you write a list or something like past tense, present tense, future tense, so I can remember?" Newby reminded her that she had already done this for her the previous semester. Blue also asked for repeats, as the other deaf tutees did, but this was more of an issue of *communication* than of directing behavior. I wonder whether it is a factor of the individual tutee's personality or the nature of the tutorial relationship that allows a tutee to be comfortable directing the tutor's behavior.

Monitoring.   Monitoring usually involved the tutor ensuring that the tutee met the expectations of the teacher and the discipline. I take this term from the British concept of a monitor, an advanced student who assists other students and upholds the teachers' expectations. Gustav stated quite clearly that as a tutor he had a certain responsibility to the professors: "If we're helping the student write a paper that's inappropriate to the assignment, it's going to be counterproductive." For each paper assignment that he worked on with Kali, he asked to see the assignment sheet and made sure that her paper met the requirements. Of the three tutoring sessions I observed with Rae and John, only one was specifically about a paper. John asked about the assignment, what she had written, and her plans for revision. John monitored Rae's writing by comparing what she had written to what was on the teacher's assignment sheet:

> John: OK, another thing I noticed, too, was . . . the first question
>   is . . . "What makes a good history book? Is good history nearer
>   to science or to literature? Do history books go out of date and
>   become useless?" OK, so, you just answered that in a sense by
>   saying that the book was a hundred years old and starting to
>   become out of date and a little useless to a contemporary reader.
> Rae: OK, oh. Should I put that in?
> John: Oh, absolutely. Yeah. You'd probably want to directly answer
>   that question and then also the question "Is good history nearer
>   to science or to literature?" . . . as opposed to answering what
>   makes a good history book and then giving your opinion about
>   what a good history book is.

Newby also monitored for the teacher's expectations. When working with Blue, they spent a lot of time trying to decipher the teacher's messy handwriting in his comments and even asked the interpreter and me for help. Blue said the handwriting did not matter—that she would just ask the teacher what it said when she saw him. Blue and Newby mostly worked on lower-order concerns, as with the Janet Jackson presentation, which had already been given. In the other papers she wrote (one about a spelling bee and another about an observation she did at a train station), they mostly corrected errors the teacher had commented on, thereby upholding the teacher's expectations. Newby checked to make sure that Blue had done the assignment correctly. She also did this with Squirt.

John also monitored with Shareef and Herrodrick. John asked to see Herrodrick's assignment and read it aloud before they began talking about it. With Shareef, John read aloud from the assignment, and then Shraeef explained it: "Basically . . . the last paper was about someone else, like an expertise [*sic*]. Like someone professional. This time we're focusing on ourselves. So, it's the same type of thing, the same idea, but we just have to—" By letting Shareef explain the assignment in his own words, John allowed him to "make it his own" and gain a better understanding of it.

Relationship of Monitoring to Tutor Training

As I conducted this study I was surprised that the tutors took such an active role supporting the teachers' assignments, the authority, and expectations. I had ideally expected to see the tutee be the one to suggest they follow the assignment or to ensure the teacher's requirements were being met, but it was almost always the tutor who brought up this topic. This is perhaps because two of the three tutors in the study are professional (i.e., with a master's degree), not peer, tutors. I had expected that the students would explain the requirements of the assignment to the tutor, and some did, but every tutor without exception advocated for the authority of the teacher. In only one instance did the tutor and the tutee deliberately subvert the teacher's authority, and this was in a tutorial with the only peer tutor in the study. This happened when John and Rae decided to use the Internet for research, which ran counter to the teacher's wishes. (Since then I have found out from my own students that using the Internet to avoid reading the textbook is a common practice.)

Perhaps this phenomenon of advocating for the teacher's assignment has to do with tutor training. Tutors at Stanhope are trained in semesterly meetings and sessions. They are also given a handbook of procedures, and they watch the video series *The Tutor's Guide* (1986). Since Stanhope's center is an academic assistance center, not a writing center, the tutor training is more general and does not focus specifically on writing. In the training manual, tutors are encouraged to check the student's syllabus "to determine what needs to be completed," which is analogous to checking the assignment sheet.

Davis's tutor training is a little more involved. There, the tutors take a semester-long tutor-training course. They are also given a packet of readings that includes these materials:

- "Early Writing Centers: Toward a History" (Carino 1995)
- "The Idea of a Writing Center" (North 1984a)
- "Collaboration, Control, and the Idea of a Writing Center" (Lunsford 1991)
- "Minimalist Tutoring: Making the Student Do All the Work" (Brooks 1991)
- "Peer Tutoring: A Contradiction in Terms?" (Trimbur 1987)
- "Rethinking Writing Center Conferencing Strategies for the ESL Writer" (Powers 1993)
- "Learning Disabilities in the Writing Center" (Neff 1994)

All of these articles were reprinted in *The Allyn and Bacon Guide to Writing Center Theory and Practice* (2001). The packet also contains a selection from the introduction of *Talking about Writing* (Clark 1985) and a selection on tutor roles from *Teaching One-to-One: The Writing Conference* (Harris 1986). In addition, tutors get a writing center handbook that details the expectations for a tutoring session at Davis. Tutors are told to be collaborators, not teachers. The handbook contains a hierarchy of concerns to work on with the student. These are divided into "global concerns" and "cosmetic concerns." The global concerns are "invention" (Does the writer have an idea what to write?), purpose (Does the writer respond to the assignment?), focus (Does the writer have an overarching point?), logic (Is the writer's logic clear?), organization (Is there a sense of organization in the essay?), and "development" (Does the writer provide explanation, description, examples?). The "cosmetic concerns" are sentence complexity, sentence clarity, language, punctuation, documentation, and spelling. So, checking to see whether the paper fulfills the requirements of the assignment is a part of the consultant's training.

In addition, consultants at Davis are taught what to do if a student comes in without a draft. This is interesting, as in the observations I saw tutors doing many of these things. Here is a list of questions from the tutor handbook to ask in such a situation:

- Do the writers simply mean that they have no draft (there may be an assignment)?
- Do the writers have work for a class other than the one they primarily come to the Center for?
- Do the writers have reading for an assignment that can be discussed and summarized/analyzed through writing?
- Are there areas in an earlier essay, perhaps one already graded, to return to?
- Do the writers keep journals or notebooks that can be fruitful for discussing writing?
- Do the writers have any nonschool writing to discuss? (*Davis College Writing Center Handbook* 2000–2001)

I saw all of these activities being practiced in my observations at Davis, except for the discussion of notebooks and journals. As an added note, here is an excerpt from the description of the duties of a tutor that is given to students when they first sign up for tutoring at Davis: "Consultants do not proofread, edit, or correct your papers—they do listen, question, comment, provide feedback, share experience and knowledge, make suggestions—they help you learn to recognize both strengths and weaknesses in your writing." The tutors at Davis for the most part live up to this.

Text-Based Taking Charge

Tutors and tutees manipulated actual text in order to improve the students' writing and making use of source materials. This taking charge of student writing and source texts includes finding and correcting errors in student texts and physically and conceptually working with written material such as handbooks, handouts, and class textbooks.

Finding and Correcting Errors

Many writing centers post signs stating, "We don't proofread" and "We are not an editing service," but these policies are irrelevant in the actual tutoring session, where finding and correcting errors happens almost every time and with almost every student. In all of the tutoring dyads I observed, there was at least one instance in which the tutor found an error and related to the student either a correction, an explanation or example, or simply a comment that the error was there. In some of the sessions tutees found and corrected their own errors; for instance, Shareef and Blue both did this. Sometimes the tutor would model a fix or a correction process.

Gustav exhibited a different technique in that he asked permission to write on Kali's paper, and that permission was granted. Rather than read the paper aloud with her, Gustav read the paper to himself, making marks, either before or during the session and then explained his marks and corrections to Kali. Even though her responses were minimal, they clearly indicated that she was actively engaged. In an interview she stated that she appreciated the way Gustav tutored and that she was "satisfied with the feedback." Although I did not observe a tutoring session with Gustav and a hearing student, he reported that he used this approach with hearing students as well and that he read aloud only about half the time, not according to whether the student was deaf or hearing but according to the length of the paper or his own mood. When I asked Gustav in an interview if he had ever done anything counter to his training when tutoring a deaf student, he replied as follows:

Gustav: [O]ne thing that we're warned about is not to be a proofreading service. . . . You don't want a student to come in and you just correct their mistakes and don't tell them what the mistakes are or give them any direction . . . to avoid those mistakes in the future. With someone who is deaf, I'm a little bit more likely to write something on the paper so they can see me as I do it and mark exactly what's going to change. . . . I try to avoid doing that too much even in those circumstances because you can still err in the direction of just proofreading.

Rebecca: Yeah.

Gustav: I'm a little bit more likely to do that with a student who's deaf.

Rebecca: [F]or ESL students as well, there needs to be a little bit more direction, maybe a little bit more editing and proofreading, and for some [tutors] that I've talked to . . . when working with deaf students, [they] will feel guilty because—or ESL as well—because they're doing . . . too much.

Gustav: [A]s far as those [go], sometimes I will make a mark anyway for a student. . . . I won't correct it, but I might circle a point of error, so that I . . . [can] remember when I'm done reading the paper to go back to it and say, "This is where one mistake is."

Rebecca: And then you ask them to try to identify the error, and then if they can't, then you offer the explanation?

Gustav: It depends. If someone is at a lower level . . . I might actually say, "Here is an example of this rule."

Rebecca: OK.

Gustav: You know, "You have two independent clauses, you've [got] a conjunction, so you should use a comma here." I might say that the first time. And then if I find another example of that in the paper, I will say, "Given what you know now, how would you approach this sentence differently?"

Rebecca: Because it is unfair to expect students to know something that they don't know.

Gustav has a good point here when he mentions that with a deaf student he is "a little bit more likely to write something on the paper so they can see me as I do it and mark exactly what's going to change." This visually oriented technique is supported by the idea that compositionists (and tutors) need to concern themselves more with visual literacies (Schriver 1992).

Newby attempted to adhere to a nondirective technique with Blue. She would usually find and point out an error and let Blue correct it herself:

Newby: [reading] "She was four year old." How many years?

Blue: -s. [fixes it]

At times Blue was confused, as in the exchange about the pronoun ("wanted her for a job," p. 81), whereas at other times she could find and correct her own errors, as when she went through her paper, adding capital letters where needed.

John helped Shareef to correct his errors in this traditional way as well. John read through Shareef's paper, sometimes asking Shareef to read problematic sentences to "hear" his mistakes. Then John usually offered a short explanation of the error. This technique may prove problematic with deaf students, although Storm (1987), from Clarke School for the Deaf, an oral school, recommends that deaf students read their compositions aloud. Nevertheless, Shareef, a hearing speaker of a nonstandard dialect, mentioned in an interview that he finds his errors better visually than aurally:

> You don't hear your mistakes when you're talkin'. I mean . . . you don't write the same way. When I'm reading, and I'm talking it . . . I hear it, "OK, it's right, it's right." That's the way I'm saying it, right, but I'm not writing it right, you know. But when I read it, I can catch it.

What he has written, even though incorrect on paper, sounds all right to Shareef in his dialect. However, his familiarity with the look of print enables him to find his errors visually. Deaf students should also be encouraged to correct their papers in this way. When Newby and John read papers with Blue and Shareef, respectively, it was the tutor who found the error and the student who corrected it after prompting. Sometimes it took a few prompts for the student to catch on, and sometimes the tutor gave the correction. Sometimes the tutee would find and correct the error without assistance, as when John read and Shareef corrected errors directly on the paper without any prompting from John.

Even though errors may not be the focus of the conference, tutors will be distracted by any errors while reading for meaning. All of the tutors experienced this. Papers with teachers' comments lend themselves to line-by-line analysis in the tutoring session (Haas 1986), but this was not borne out in Herrodrick's and Squirt's sessions when they brought a draft with such comments to the session. In Rae's, Herrodrick's, and

Squirt's sessions, errors were dealt with by happenstance. The focus of the tutorial was not error, but when their tutors noticed an error, they would mention it in passing. For instance, in a session that focused mostly on meaning and idea development, Newby mentioned that Squirt had a lot of run-on sentences but did not stop to correct them. In a subsequent tutoring session, which also focused on literary analysis, Newby suggested that Squirt take out an "and" and replace it with a period to break up a long sentence. They also talked about the subjunctive and the use of quotes. Newby suggested that Squirt look in her handbook for the guidelines on quoting and directed her to format and cite a long quote correctly. Errors were mentioned offhand and not corrected in the tutoring session. Newby appeared confident that Squirt could later correct the errors on her own and that error was not to be the main focus of the session; rather, she briefly mentioned the errors and then moved on.

In the first session I observed with Herrodrick and John, Herrodrick had gotten a draft of his paper back with his teacher's comments. Most of these concerns were substantive, having to do with the rhetorical strength of his argument. At several points, John commented that Herrodrick had no grammatical concerns he needed to work on in his writing. John mentioned some of the mechanical concerns that the teacher had marked, but much as Squirt and Newby interacted, neither John nor Herrodrick offered a fix for the errors. The errors were mentioned almost casually; for example, when John noticed an error the teacher had marked, he said, "This is something that would slip past me."

Only one of the sessions that I observed with Rae focused on a student-written text. Rae brought a paper to the tutoring session that the teacher had not yet commented on. As John read through Rae's draft on the computer screen, he became distracted by syntactic concerns. He noticed an infelicitous sentence and became confused. In order to clarify it, he asked her to explain what the book was about and who wrote it. After Rae had done so, he was able to understand what she meant and offer a solution. When Rae suggested they just take out the nonrestrictive element John explained:

You just put it in as long as you have commas here. That's fine. 'The author was a doctor by profession and he, like his protagonist, lived in a small villiage." That's a fine sentence. You know it's a non-restrictive element because if you omit it, it still would sound correct.

John went on to give a detailed explanation of nonrestrictive elements, complete with example.

Orlando, Gramly, and Hoke (1997) recommend editing and proof-reading help for deaf writers, which seemingly runs counter to traditional writing center practice. However, by refusing editing and proofreading to nonmainstream students, writing center practitioners are privileg-ing those who are already members of the dominant discourse (Grimm 1999). In fact, by not proofreading, tutors may even be violating the legal rights of students with disabilities (Hodge and Preston-Sabin 1997).

I expected to see tutors do some editing and proofreading for deaf students, and I did. Since this goes against their training, I anticipated that they would feel uncomfortable doing so (Blau, Hall, and Sparks 2002), and, indeed, John apologized every time he mentioned grammar. Gustav, on the other hand, took a more directive role with editing and saw no problem with that. I did not see any tutors refusing to edit, although Newby used a nondirective technique that was frustrating when it did not click, yet worked well at other times. I correctly anticipated that deaf writers would see mechanical correctness as a major issue (Brueggemann 1992). Editing and grammatical corrections were accomplished through directive, nondirective, and collaborative techniques.

Although tutors are trained to be nondirective and to focus on global rather than local concerns, clearly they are often directive and engage in error finding and fixing. Deaf tutees tended to be explicit about what they wanted from the tutoring session, perhaps because the Deaf culture values direct communication or because these students were highly motivated. Sometimes nondirectiveness proved frustrating for them, again, for cultural reasons. When working with deaf students, the tutors reduced their use of the standard tutoring techniques of reading aloud and "listening for errors."

Taking Charge of Text

Taking charge refers to the manipulation and use of texts other than student-written class assignments. Tutors and tutees took charge of non-student-written text in various ways. They physically controlled books, handouts, or papers. They shared texts by reading them aloud or silently, alone or together. They, especially the tutors, also recommended texts to be used, manipulated, or enjoyed outside the tutoring session.

Handbooks.   All of the tutors in the study advocated the use of a handbook: Gustav, *The Simon and Schuster Handbook for Writers,* and Newby and John, *A Writer's Reference* (also referred to as the Hacker handbook). This is probably a result of the school's culture, as whichever handbook the English department favored was most likely the one tutors would recommend. John actually carried *A Writer's Reference* to his tutoring sessions, and in an interview Brock commented positively on that practice. However, when John tried to interest Rae in the handbook, she did not bite. Shareef, on the other hand, used his handbook often, and he and John even used it together in a session. In an interview John commented on Shareef's willingness to consult the handbook on his own, outside the tutoring session.

Handouts.   Tutors also shared handouts with the tutees. Newby shared numerous handouts with Blue, including one on verbs that she created especially for her. In the first session I observed with Blue and Newby, Newby asked her whether she had the handout and had understood it. Blue said, "Yes," but she told me later in an interview that she had not understood it. After Newby shared a number of handouts with Blue, Blue stated,

> Honestly, sometimes I look at the paper and sometimes I just don't understand it. . . . . If the person explains it . . . then I get it.

This comment demonstrates three things: (1) the investment that Newby put into tutoring that she would create a handout for a specific student's needs, (2) that students can learn only when they are ready and that exposure to the material at the wrong time will not result in learning, and (3) that materials must be presented in a different format for students with different learning needs. During one tutoring session, Kali asked Gustav for a handout. At the end of the session he brought her a whole sheaf of handouts. Kali responded, "OK. Thank you. I didn't expect all this. This is great." Another tutee would be daunted by the number of handouts Gustav shared, but Kali informed me in an interview that she is a big reader and gets a lot of her information through reading.

Class Textbooks. Tutors and tutees also shared class textbooks. Newby and Squirt discussed the paper she was writing about *Giovanni's Room,* and they passed the book back and forth, looking for examples and reading both aloud and silently. In one of Rae's sessions with John, she shared the books that she was writing about, and even critiqued them. Kali shared her textbook with Gustav when she asked him whether her poetry explication was sufficient. They read the poem in the book together and then discussed it. In one of her tutorials Blue worked on summarizing her science book.

Internet. Both Rae and Blue used printouts from the Internet in their tutorials. Rae was slightly peeved with the amount of text John printed to help her study for her Spanish history class, but in general she agreed with his action. Blue attempted to summarize a printout from the Internet for her acting class. In both of these cases, the tutees used the Internet to avoid other reading: Rae, to avoid reading her class textbooks and lecture notes, and Blue, to avoid reading a book that she was supposed to have checked out from the library.

Other Texts. I did not observe the tutees sharing books or any other materials other than class textbooks in the tutorial, although some of them shared books with me on the side. Newby gave Blue the gift of a book for pleasure reading. Although I did not observe it, I know that Herrodrick and Squirt shared their outside writing with their tutors. Herrodrick was writing a long short story or novella, and Squirt wrote a monthly youth column for a gay newspaper. I know Shareef wrote raps, but I do not know whether he shared these with John. None of the deaf tutees, however, mentioned doing any out-of-school writing.

Making Sense

Making sense is the process of understanding and learning, which is the primary focus of most tutoring sessions. The term "making sense" was prevalent throughout the data and was used at some point by almost all of the participants in their tutoring sessions and interviews. For instance, in almost every tutoring session someone asked, "Does this make sense?" Because the question was so prevalent throughout the data, I chose it as an *in vivo* code to represent the concepts of creating understanding, meaning, and learning in the tutoring sessions. It appears that sense making is a primary goal of the tutoring session, after acquiring a new discourse. In order to enter a new discourse community, people have to know whether their attempts are making sense and if they are on the right track. Tutors and tutees attempted to make sense of and through discourse and text. Making sense by conversing is the use of discourse to effectively communicate one's thoughts, to elicit another person's thoughts, or to confirm understanding either of content or of the tutoring partner's perspective. Making sense of and through text are efforts to consume or even produce texts in pursuit of the participants' goals for the session. These goals can be as simple as understanding the surface meaning or vocabulary of a text or more complex ones such as summarizing, interpreting, or evaluating a given text.

Discourse-Based Making Sense

Discourse based making sense is the use of conversation for communication and elicitation of participants' ideas and intentions in the tutoring session. This discourse-based making sense can involve making sense of the direct, content-based information required in the tutoring session or of the behavior of the other participant.

Making Sense of Information

Making sense of information is what the casual observer might think tutoring is all about: the transfer of knowledge, otherwise known as "learning." In reality, this communication is just one aspect of the multifaceted nature of the tutoring session as evidenced in these chapters. Making sense of information involves discussing ideas, explaining and asking for explanations, confirming understanding, and questioning for procedure and clarification.

Discussing Ideas. Discussing ideas, along with finding and correcting errors, is a typical, even stereotypical, tutoring activity. Gustav and Kali collaborated on brainstorming ideas on what to write about, as did John and Herrodrick, Newby and Squirt, John and Shareef, and John and Rae. Only Newby and Blue did not collaborate on ideas when I was observing, but Newby reported to me in an interview that they had done so once before. Gustav and Kali discussed her ideas for her Ray Bradbury paper and her poetry explication. John and Herrodrick had lively, collaborative discussions, first about what Herrodrick would write about, and later, what he had ended up writing about. Of the three sessions I observed with John and Shareef, half of one session was dedicated to brainstorming ideas for a text.

The collaborative nature of John and Herrodrick's discussions is evident in this exchange:

> Herrodrick: I mean, you go somewhere where you can get the money.
> John: OK.
> Herrodrick: You can live out the American dream, retire.
> John: And get away from everybody else.
> Herrodrick: Get away.

John finished Herrodrick's sentence, and Herrodrick echoed the words John used. Together they were making sense, creating meaning through their discourse. In that same session, there was an interesting use of a question. Herrodrick said, "I'm thinking . . . it's just that way here in America. Is it also that way in Europe?" I tried to make sense of this question in the following analytic memo, which also demonstrates my thought process in the analysis, coding, and arrangement of the data:

> In his tutoring session of 12/12/03, pg. 10, Herrodrick asks a perplexing question. He and John are discussing ideas for his paper and he asks [the aforementioned question]. What is this question functioning as? Does he really think that John has the answer? (taking charge/info) Is he asking himself a rhetorical question, or [is this] a conversation opener? (discussion or relating) Clarifying procedure?

No. What is the goal of this? To get the info, to get the tutor to talk, or just a musing? I think it's a discussion of ideas. (analytic memo, June 6, 2004)

As a result of this thought process I decided to include this question under "discussing ideas." The discussions between John and Herrodrick were the only exchanges in this study that were truly collaborative discussions of ideas, where the tutor and tutee freely shared ideas. The main difference between the dyad of John and Herrodrick and the others is that they were the only pair who were truly peers in age, academic status, race/ethnicity, hearing status, and sex.

The other dyads that discussed ideas were Newby and Squirt, John and Shareef, and John and Rae. These tutoring sessions were tutor-directed elicitations of the tutee's ideas through questioning rather than collaborative discussions such as those between John and Herrodrick. By questioning Squirt, Newby tried to help her clarify and refine her ideas for her paper on *Giovanni's Room*. When John and Shareef discussed ideas for Shareef's paper, John similarly drew him out with questions that would expand his ideas for his paper: "So what was it that kind of alleviated those nerves?" John and Rae discussed Rae's ideas for her paper comparing two books. At one point in the tutorial, John read the questions from Rae's assignment, and she responded in sign language while the interpreter interpreted and John took notes. Rather than discussing ideas, there was more of a one-way telling of her ideas to John. Similarly, in Kali's tutoring session, when she asked Gustav whether she had interpreted part of the poem correctly, he elicited her ideas with the following questions:

> Gustav: What is God doing, what is God saying to her, and how is he saying it, do you feel?
>
> Kali: I think that Emily sees God as a teacher.
>
> Gustav: And how does he teach?

Gustav, rather than offering his own ideas, tried to help Kali generate ideas. This elicitation of the tutee's ideas by questioning is an example of orthodox, Socratic tutoring.

Requesting and Giving Explanations. Explaining and asking for an explanation are key activities in the tutoring session. The tutees asked their tutors for information, especially when they perceived that the tutor had the answer they needed. Of course, the objective of this type of question was to direct the tutor's behavior, but I categorize it under sense making because the ultimate goal is to understand something. These are usually questions that ask the tutor for an explanation, especially of a grammatical rule. For instance, Rae asked, "What is that? Nonrestrictive element, what's that?" and then John explained:

> John: Let me give you an example. "John, who was five foot eight, was walking to school this afternoon." . . . If you started a sentence like [that], that would be a nonrestrictive [element]. . . . It's not necessarily something . . . that is important to that particular sentence. If I say, "John, who was five foot eight . . .
> Rae: Oh, OK.
> John: . . . walked to school yesterday with red gym shoes." The fact that I'm five foot eight isn't necessarily really important to the sentence. It's a nonrestrictive element, and it needs to be bracketed by commas.

All of the tutees' requests for an explanation were successful. John often modeled a sentence or referred to the handbook. In the interview after the conference, Rae indicated that she did not necessarily want long detailed explanations even though she had asked for a clarification:

> Rebecca: I noticed that John was using a grammatical term with you, and you really didn't wanna know about the grammatical term. You just wanted to know how to fix your sentence. Is that right?
> Rae: Right . . . it's like the grammar stuff I'm not so concerned about. Just fix my paper, you know, 'cause I'm not a writer, and I'm not going to become a script writer. I just want to have my papers fixed so that I can . . . get an "A."

Rae's question, "Restrictive element, what's that?" might have simply been a request for a definition of an unfamiliar term. After a long explanation, however, John said, "I don't want to focus too much on grammar," and Rae said, "I see." The irony of this statement was lost on the participants, but I noticed it as I was analyzing the data.

Tutees also elicited clarifications indirectly:

Blue: For example, when I write . . . "was looked" . . . I get confused. Because it's supposed to be past tense, but I write the wrong thing. So I need to change it to "was looking." I mean it's just so confusing . . .

Newby: Look at this [handout]. This talks about verbs. These two pages. [reads] "In the present tense verbs show action or state of being that happens at the time or occurs regularly," and then you have an example. Then you've got past tense. Simple past and then you have an example. And you've got future tense. It's got all the tenses. I'll copy this for you, this part [gives Blue paper] . . . Take a look at that. And ask any questions that you might have.

In this case, Newby used a handout that explains various tenses; in other cases, she would use an example. When the tutor noticed an error in the student's paper, the tutee would usually ask for a grammatical explanation. Sometimes a deaf tutee would bring up a grammar point that the tutor had not necessarily mentioned. Of all of the tutees in the study, only Kali and Blue initiated discussion on grammatical issues. In other cases it was usually the tutor who would do so, usually in response to something in the students' papers.

Both Kali and Blue raised a question about article usage. Obviously, articles are on the minds of deaf learners. and they have been written about as a point of difficulty (Brueggemann 1992; Kelly 1987). My own sign language teacher, who, I believe, was teaching us PSE, told us not to use articles in our signing. In one session, Newby gave Blue a handout on articles and asked her to read it and ask any questions she might have. After Blue had read it she said, "I'm curious, 'a' and 'an.' I know 'a' means like 'a person'—one person, but 'an'? 'An'?" Newby then gave her an explanation based on spelling rather than sound, which will work most, but not all, of the time. In one of Kali's tutoring sessions, she asked Gustav to explain articles: "I know the paper needs help in English—the use of the word 'the,'" and Gustav went on to give her an explanation.

I did not observe any hearing tutees asking for grammatical explanations. The fact that Herrodrick did not do so likely has to do with the fact that, as John explained, Herrodrick never has "a recurring grammatical thing that we need to talk about. [His] grammar's fine for the most part." Herrodrick and John did not talk about grammar or mechanics in their tutoring sessions except when John pointed out a few teacher comments, and Herrodrick just answered with "yeah" and "OK." Shareef did not ask for any explanations, either, but, without being prompted, John offered a short clarification after each grammatical fix.

Confirming Understanding

Every tutoring dyad worked to confirm understanding. Both tutors and tutees wanted to know whether their contributions made sense. Ted, the director of Stanhope's Academic Assistance Center, said in an interview that, when tutoring a deaf student, he frequently checks for understanding by asking the student to put the material in their own words. But most of the sense-making questions between tutor and tutees that I observed were simple yes–or–no questions. For instance, John asked Rae, "Do you know what I mean?" as a genuine question rather than as a pause filler, and earlier in the same session Rae had asked John, "What do you mean?" Meaning is an integral component of understanding and making sense. A person must know what another person's utterance means in order to understand and make sense out of it. Rae asked John to read her paper to "make sure it makes sense." She also said, "If a paragraph doesn't make sense . . . you can edit it." In addition, at the end of her longest turn in the session, in which Rae explained her feelings about relations between the United States and Latin America, she asked, "Does that make sense?" In addition, Newby often asked Blue, "Makes sense?" in their tutoring sessions. Newby also used the technique Ted described earlier in the tutoring session with Blue, when they were summarizing the science book:

Newby: So, now you understand?
Blue: I understand, yeah.
Newby: OK. Well, tell us.

In this way, Blue had to demonstrate that she actually understood the material by putting it in her own words. Understanding is important to Blue in her own writing. In an interview she talked about her writing being "pretty good" because it is "pretty understandable." When writing is not good, "other people can't understand or make sense of [it]."

Questioning for Procedure and Clarification.   Making sense involves asking questions to gain information needed to proceed with the tutoring session. Newby asked factual questions of Blue for which only Blue had the answer. For example, when referring to a printout they were working with, Newby asked, "Is this all that we took off the Internet?" When Newby asked Squirt about her writing for publication, Squirt clarified for understanding: "You mean for the [local gay newspaper]?" Squirt also asked a question for clarification when Newby said, "I want you to tell me," and she replied by asking, "Tell you what?" John also asked Rae genuine questions for which only she had the answers, such as, "Flashcards— did you make the flashcards?" These are procedural questions.

When a tutor asked nondirective questions to draw out the tutee, as when Newby asked, "Why is David so confused?" it is not to inform the tutor but rather to assist the writer in knowing what to write in order to develop the paper. When Gustav asked Kali, "The Dandelion Crater, is that on the moon?" it is not clear whether he really did not know the answer or whether he was indicating that her description should be more explicit. This is a case of an ambiguous question.

Gustav also asked purely procedural questions like "What are the length requirements for this paper?" In fact, most tutors asked both hearing and deaf tutees how long the paper had to be. In addition, Newby asked Squirt, "When did you write this—last week?" John asked Shareef, "Do you still have to turn this in?" and he asked Herrodrick, "When's the last time you saw [a Trix commercial]?" These important questions help the tutor to make sense of the situation so they can best assist the tutee. Some tutees asked procedural questions in order to understand what was going on. For instance, Rae asked John, "What was that question for? [pointing to the notes] The one you just wrote? What was I answering?"

Trying to figure out what her teacher meant by his comments, Blue asked, "Am I supposed to write in the past tense?" Because Blue was trying to elicit direction from the tutor on how to proceed, this was a procedural rather than a take-charge question. When Gustav told Kali about the volumes of short-story criticism in the reference section of the library, Kali asked, "Where can I find that?" When Gustav asked her where she would like to start, she replied, "So you mean this part right here?"

Shareef also asked such questions to clarify procedure. He sometimes echoed John's words to make sure he understood correctly. For instance, when John told him the paper had to contain four thousand words, he replied, "Is it four thousand?" and when John told him that the following Tuesday was the sixteenth, Shareef responded, "It's next Tuesday?" These were procedural/clarifying questions. Tutees Squirt and Herrodrick did not ask any questions of this type.

Making Sense of Behavior

Making sense of behavior involves using discourse to understand the reason for another's behavior. For this study, the only tutoring dyad who directly made sense of behavior was Squirt and Newby. Specifically, Squirt was the only tutee who engaged in problematic behavior during the study, and Newby attempted to make sense out of it by asking her questions. In addition, as a mature tutor, Newby likely felt comfortable directly confronting Squirt about her behavior. For example, when Squirt was acting contrary at one point, the following exchange took place:

Newby: Squirt, what's the matter with you today?
Squirt: I just don't want to do it.
Newby: Then why did you come?
Squirt: I don't know, to have you do it.

Later in the session, Newby surmised that Squirt was uncomfortable with the camera or with the observation, but Squirt denied that the camera was bothering her, and when I asked her whether I should leave, she told me to stay. Through later interviews with Squirt and her mother I learned that Squirt's learning disability had likely caused her to feel frustrated.

Text-Based Making Sense

Text-based making sense refers to the use of printed texts and of writing to comprehend important concepts. Tutors and tutees made sense of texts by reading, writing, and evaluating them.

Reading for Understanding, Analysis, and Interpretation

Tutors and tutees often read texts and concentrated on simple understanding of content or on more sophisticated tasks like analysis and interpretation, especially when working on writing and reading assignments.

Understanding. Sometimes text-based making sense was as straightforward as reading for simple, literal understanding. For instance, Blue's writing teacher had extremely bad handwriting, so part of each session on teacher-commented papers involved trying to read the teacher's comments. Also, Blue tried to make sense out of the science book she had to summarize, but she did not understand the vocabulary. Because she had trouble making meaning from text, she preferred to get an explanation from the interpreter rather than reading a handout or a dictionary. She wanted to learn vocabulary, but she was frustrated, as she told me in an interview:

> I wanna learn more vocabulary words. Those big words, those tough words that I want to get. That's why I get so frustrated. I hate to read books. I'm so sick of those big words that I can't understand. It bores me.

Rae also made sense of text when she and John discussed the books she was writing about. Writing was actually helping her make sense of reading since her assignment was to compare two books. She used her lack of understanding of one of the books to support the point of her paper. Rae and John also tried to make sense of text when they were looking for information on the Internet to help Rae study for her final exam. With Shareef and Herrodrick, the only texts they made sense of, guided by John, were the teacher's assignment sheets.

Interpreting and Analyzing. Squirt and Newby attempted to make sense of *Giovanni's Room* by interpreting it. They passed the text back and forth, reading both aloud and silently, and came to understand this text together. Their goal was to find examples that Squirt could use in her literary analysis paper. Kali and Gustav also made sense of text in more than a simple, literal way when they discussed her interpretation of Dickinson's poem "Some Keep the Sabbath Going to Church." In order to explicate the poem, Kali had to read beyond the surface forms of the words to grasp the writer's intent. Rae analyzed her history books for her comparison paper. She needed not only to understand the books but also to compare them in her analysis, which is a higher-order task. The other tutees did not interpret or analyze texts.

Writing

Sense making through writing is actual composing during the tutoring session with the goal of increased comprehension of the content or task. For instance, Squirt made sense by composing when she wrote down the ideas she and Newby were generating. Rae also composed for meaning with John as she added ideas to her paper as they were generated in the conference. Blue could be seen writing summaries of the material she brought to the tutoring conference, both from the science book and an Internet printout on acting. Although it was extremely difficult for her to put the material into her own words, she began to make sense of the material by writing it. In turn, John wrote down the ideas that Rae was generating in their tutoring session. Shareef also made sense of his ideas by writing during the conference. In one session I observed, John gave Shareef extended time to compose in order to capture his thoughts. John reported that he usually did this with Shareef. Kali and Gustav did not do any extended composing in the sessions I observed. They wrote only to correct errors or to take brief notes. Herrodrick and John did not do any extended writing, either, but Herrodrick did take some notes as they were generating ideas.

Evaluating

People sometimes attempt to make sense of texts by evaluating them. In this study this usually involved the tutee evaluating the course text. Rae evaluated hers in the paper she was writing: "To me it seemed really bland and boring." Analyses and critiques are types of text evaluations. I observed Blue evaluating the book that she was summarizing when she said, "It's over my head" and "I don't understand." She also communicated her evaluation of the book nonverbally, by looks and gestures of confusion and frustration. Kali's only evaluation of her source text was also confusion: "This is a little bit hard for me to understand . . . I wasn't really sure of the interpretation of that part. It wasn't clear." Most of the deaf tutees' negative evaluations of their textbooks had to do with lack of comprehension.

Squirt said, "This is stupid," but it was not clear whether she was evaluating the novel, the assignment, or her paper. I do not think she was passing judgment on the tutoring situation, as both she and Newby told me in their interviews that they had a good relationship. Squirt evaluated the text in her draft: "It was a sad book. . . . I like the book because . . ." She did like the book and she liked to read, as she told me later in an interview. However, as she was looking through the book, she implicitly evaluated it or perhaps just showed her frustration with the task when she asked, "Where's the stinkin' chapter?" She also assessed the book explicitly in her talk: "It's too long" (it was 150 pages), and "It wasn't vague enough" (she meant it was too vague). Herrodrick and Shareef did not evaluate their course texts, most probably because they were in writing classes that were not based on textbooks.

INTERLUDE

———

Interpreters

Linda

Linda is an interpreter and instructor at Davis College. She is in her twenties, white, and hearing. She has been interpreting for six years and has interpreted quite a few tutoring sessions in writing and has also done both general educational interpreting in a classroom situation and "platform interpreting," which is for a public performance. She is quite aware of and sensitive to the ethical issues surrounding the tutoring session and the linguistic and cultural issues that arise when deaf and hearing people interact. She has an informational sheet that she distributes to the hearing tutor or professor beforehand, providing some pointers on the interpretation process. In the actual tutoring session, she is careful not to add anything of her own but to remain neutral, a conduit for communication. She will stop the session, however, if she does not understand something.

We spoke about some of the issues related to interpreting a tutoring session in writing for a deaf student. She said that "hopefully the interpreter's doing a good job, you know, [if not], it could really destroy the session." She continued:

> I think that that's important that the deaf student feels comfortable, as well as the tutor, as well as the interpreter, because they are part of

the dynamic. And also . . . to the other extreme in that situation, I've heard of interpreters who are in tutoring sessions where the tutor doesn't know what they're talking about. And the interpreter's sitting there going, 'That's not right!' and sort of altering the interpretation of what the tutor's saying.

Of course it is against the interpreter's job description and code of ethics to change anything, so in this case the interpreter deviated from the job description and the code of ethics in order not to give the tutee inaccurate information. Linda went on to explain: "I've had conversations with tutors, with interpreters: what do you do in that situation? You just have to do your job even though you know the information you are relaying is [incorrect]."

Linda explained the language issue in detail:

When there's conversation happening in the tutoring session, I use whatever language preference the deaf person has. So, some deaf students are obviously more ASL than others. So in that, for the conversational part of the tutoring session, I'm using their preference. When it comes to actually putting it in words, I tend to do a lot of fingerspelling, a lot of—I don't know Signed English. Signed Exact English [SEE]. So when it comes to how you sign -ing and -ed and -ness, and all of that stuff, I make it up. . . . I tend to just fingerspell. . . . I was never trained in that . . . but I do use as much of that as I possibly can when it comes to them actually taking from what they see coming off of my hands and putting it on paper. Often teachers will write a lot. And even though I'm there as an interpreter, it makes more sense for them to actually be writing what they want the deaf person to be getting because . . . you eliminate me in the process then, and you eliminate that possibility for misinterpretation.

It should be quite obvious that Linda is a highly skilled and reflective interpreter. In fact, she has taught classes in interpreting at Davis.

Jay

Jay is a young black woman who is a graduate of Davis College's interpreter-training program. She works full time at the college as an interpreter and at the time of the study had three years of experience in this role. She is familiar with sign language and Deaf culture because she has a deaf aunt and uncle. She began taking classes because she wanted to learn more about sign language. She found she liked it, so she changed her major from music business management to interpreting. In addition to educational interpreting, she has done theatrical and platform interpreting. She has passed the State Assessment Screening and is preparing for her Registry of Interpreters for the Deaf (RID) certification.

Jay noted that most of the deaf writers in her interpreting sessions concentrated on "grammar and content," especially "[t]he structure of English sentences" and "the content of what's being discussed in class, [such as] an in-class assignment." She thinks it is important to note how difficult it is for deaf people to learn English since they have no input from spoken language. She also mentioned that time could be a factor in the interpreted tutoring session since the communication takes place in a "triangle."

Regarding tutoring deaf college students, Jay suggests that the best method would be to have tutors who knew sign language: "if they knew how to communicate with them in their own language, I think . . . a lot more could be done." This could also alleviate some of the "time issues." In addition, Jay believes tutors should be aware of the extra effort that deaf students have to expend just to do the same work that comes easily to hearing students. Jay mentioned that deaf students need to put in "triple the effort" of their hearing classmates and that "unless they [do so], I don't think they're ever going to be really successful at mastering the English language." This is not a negative comment about deaf people. It is just Jay's observation of how hard deaf people have to work to learn to write English. Tutors need to be aware of this and not become frustrated. Jay explained:

> Some tutors . . . get so frustrated because, you know, we just went over this same thing . . . it's a simple concept. We went over [it] for an hour, and then you come back, and it's the same problem. One tutor was just so frustrated. And I felt bad because I wanted to explain it to him that you just have to be patient with them, but he just got so frustrated: "How are you not understanding this concept?"

Tutors need to have patience with deaf students.

For other interpreters who will be interpreting a tutoring session in writing with a deaf college student, Jay suggests that they be "skilled with ASL and transliterating." She explained that the interpreter must match the students' language choice during the tutoring session. Since Jay works full time at the college, she is already familiar with many of the students she interprets for. However, if she were scheduled to work with someone she did not know, she would "try to get here a little earlier and just . . . chat with them a bit just to see . . . [whether] they use ASL, or is it pretty much English, or is it a mix of both? And then you . . . try to match what they . . . put out there." In some cases the educational or the communicative aspect will demand one or the other (i.e., ASL or English). In most tutoring sessions, according to Jay, "from what I've seen there's a mix of signed English and ASL going on."

Melissa

Melissa is a part-time interpreter at Stanhope College. She is a white woman in her forties and the mother of a deaf son. Some of her friends are interpreters, and they encouraged her to try interpreting profession-ally. Originally she had not planned to be an educational interpreter, but the college needed help, so she filled in. Now she loves it. Before this she had done stage and medical interpreting. She is a kind and gentle woman who is very easygoing yet serious.

Before the sessions with Kali, she had not interpreted for a tutoring session in writing. She is registered with the state as an interpreter but, at the time of the study, had not yet acquired her national certification. Melissa mentioned that "in the school setting [there is] very little inter-preting. It's mostly transliterating." This means that the interpreter often transliterates word for word from spoken to signed English rather than translating from English to ASL and back. She said, "I'm comfortable with both, but I am more comfortable with the transliterating. I feel that's more my strength. And I'm doing that day in [and] day out." She went on to explain, as Jay did, that "our responsibility is . . . [when] on any given job . . . we should arrive there early so we can communicate with the deaf person and see are they more ASL or are they more English? And then we should match [their language usage]."

At home she uses both ASL and English with her deaf son, "but he gets ASL in school." She also said that he has been exposed to "deaf children and deaf adults . . . since he was a baby. . . . I'd have to say he's more advanced because he was born hearing, but at five months he became deaf, and a good friend of mine was an interpreter. She took care of him while I worked." Melissa believes that exposure to signed language at a young age was very beneficial to her son. She thinks that students who do not have this exposure may fall behind, and that concerns her.

CHAPTER 5

⁓

Interpersonal Factors

W HILE CONDUCTING MY grounded-theory research, I discovered that the other factors influencing tutoring were mostly interpersonal—the way in which the participants related to each other during the sessions. These relational factors include the effectiveness of various communication models, the role of affect, the discourse features the participants used, the participants' personal qualities, various cultural factors, and learning disability.

Communication

One of my original research questions concerned communication: "How do the various communication models work between a hearing tutor and a deaf tutee, and in what situations, if any, is a particular communication model preferable?" Of all the possible communication models for tutoring writing with deaf students, I was able to include only the use of sign language interpreters in the present study. Tutoring that involves deaf students and hearing tutors who do not know sign language can also take place by writing in English, either on computers or on paper, but I was not fortunate enough to be able to include such tutorials in my data set.

Even though all of the sessions in the main data set were conducted through interpreters, writing either on paper or on computer (depending, of course, on the tutee's preference) is also a valid way to tutor.

I had permission to observe at a site where tutors and tutees communicated live by typing together on a computer but was unable to make any observations there. I did get to observe one tutorial at a different college conducted in writing on paper, but the participant did not wish to continue with the observations, so in the end I was able to study only tutoring conducted through interpreters. In this section I discuss the factors influencing communication, such as the use of interpreters, the participants' physical orientation, the use of technology for communication, and miscommunication in tutorials with deaf tutees and hearing tutors who do not know sign language.

Interpreters

Interestingly, few articles in the writing center literature on tutoring deaf students discusses the use of an interpreter (exceptions are Nash 2008, Schmidt et al. 2009, Babcock 2011, and Davis and Smith 2000), yet in a previous study (Day 2002) and in the present study many, if not most, deaf/hearing writing center tutorials take place with interpreters present. The use of an interpreter in higher education is fairly common (Mindess 1999). Although required by the Americans with Disabilities Act, the use of an interpreter could be problematic for a few reasons. Even though it is against the law not to provide interpreters when necessary, some institutions do not have the financial resources to pay them. I have spoken informally with writing center directors who report that, for this reason, they do not use interpreters. In addition, hearing students who are speakers of other languages are not generally provided with native-language interpreters in the writing conference, which is usually conducted in the target language of English as a form of comprehensible input (Krashen 1982) and for oral/aural reinforcement of correct forms. Of course, deaf students usually cannot engage in oral/aural processing of English, so the comprehensible input must be in writing. Sign language input from an interpreter is either in ASL or a signed modality of English that may present incomplete input (PSE or contact signing). None of the interpreters or deaf participants in the study used SEE I, SEE II, or any other coded English sign system.

Another issue in using a sign language interpreter is that the tutee's voice is not represented because the word choice in English is that of the interpreter, not the tutee, unless the tutee fingerspells. Deaf study participant Kali fingerspells often, as she is concerned with precise word choice in English, and fingerspelling is the only way to exactly represent English in sign. The reason for this is that a particular sign can have multiple meanings in English, or a single English word can have multiple signs, depending on shades of meaning. With regard to precise word choice, when a tutor and a tutee are working on reading comprehension, often the tutee will read a passage, and then the tutor will ask the tutee to put the reading into the tutee's own words. When working through an interpreter, this becomes complicated:

Blue:	I don't know what "desire" means.
Newby:	[to Jay] Are you telling her?
Jay [interpreter]:	I was just showing her the sign for it.
Blue:	It's like [signs]
Jay:	Spell what you just said.
Blue:	It means you're . . . eager.
Jay:	The interpretation is really wack right now . . .
Blue:	You need to want it.
Newby:	There you go. . . . You're eager for something, or you want it really badly.
	. . .
Jay:	I'm trying to get her to give me the word, not the word I just gave her. That would be my interpretation of the word.

When Blue did not understand a word in the reading, Jay gave her the sign in explanation, as the fingerspelling would not do any good—it would be the same information she was receiving from the page. But the problem with showing her the sign is that the paraphrase is no longer the tutee's words but the interpreter's. Jay explicitly evaluated the difficulty in the interpretation ("[It's] really wack"). In Blue's case, if she did not know the word, she could not paraphrase the sentence. The dictionary would not help either; Blue explained that if she looked a word up in the dictionary, she still could not understand the meaning because she did not understand the English definition. If the interpreter gives a sign gloss for the word, then the tutee has not done the work of putting the passage into her own words. Barnes (2006) also mentions the issues of paraphrasing and interpreted tutoring sessions. Perhaps a way to get around this problem is for the interpreter or the tutor to explain the meaning of the word in such a way that the target sign is not used, much like an ESL teacher explains a new word entirely in English without using the word itself. Alternatively, the tutee could write the paraphrase instead of signing it.

The interpreters in this study attempted to remain neutral and valued their role as conduits for communication. The interpreter would intervene only in the event of a misunderstanding or a miscommunication in order to clarify what each party meant. As Linda put it, "Interpreters are not teachers, advocates, tutors, friends, or helpers of the deaf student. Simply communication facilitators." Although I did not observe it in my study, Linda says that in an educational context an interpreter will sometimes "ask a teacher for captions on a video, for better sight lines, for written information, and so on. In many cases, this is also advocating for the interpreter so that that person can do a better job." I did not observe interpreters advocating for students in any way; if anyone did this, it was the tutor. For instance, Newby helped Blue get registered for a class she needed.

At Davis College, interpreters would hand out an information sheet to the tutors or instructors they worked with. The tip that applies most to the tutoring session is as follows:

Deaf students should be addressed in the first person. The interpreter is not a representative for the deaf student or the deaf community. When needing to communicate with the student, [tutors] should *not* use phrases like "Tell him . . ." or "Ask her . . ." No questions should be directed to the interpreter him/herself unless the question is in regard to information conveyed or flow of . . . speech.

Other tips relevant to the tutoring sessions are that the interpreter should receive materials that will be discussed in advance, that the deaf student should be held to "the same educational expectations as other students," and that the interpreter should not be expected to participate at all in the proceedings but simply be there to facilitate communication. The information sheet also explains that interpreters at Davis follow the Registry of Interpreters for the Deaf code of ethics. The interpreters in this study did not have any special training for working in a tutoring session. Linda explained, "We are thrown into a variety of settings where anything can occur, and rarely is an interpreter trained in those areas."

Physical Orientation

The use of an interpreter raises physical issues, such as where to sit and whom to address. In many of the tutoring sessions I observed, the tutor and the tutee sat next to each other, while the interpreter sat opposite them. For instance, when John and Rae worked on the computer, they would sit side by side in front of the monitor, and Linda would sit to the side, facing them. This setup worked well. Occasionally Linda would have to lean forward to see what was on the computer screen. However, in an interview, Rae said she would rather have the interpreter and the tutor sit side by side so she could maintain eye contact with both. However, this setup will not work when both tutor and tutee need to see the computer screen and the tutee needs to see the interpreter. When Blue and Newby worked with Jay, generally they would sit next to each other, and Jay would sit opposite them. This worked well because Blue liked it when she and Newby could have the paper between them and look at it together. In an interview Blue told me, "I remember we were sitting next to each other, and I really appreciate that. Next to each other for communication." When I then asked her whether she would recommend this technique to tutors who would be working with deaf students, she replied as follows:

> I would suggest that [the tutor] sit next to the student with the paper. Show each other the errors and make the corrections together. It's a better understanding when the deaf student can sit next to the tutor and see what's going on in their paper.

This setup would indicate that the tutor and tutee are sitting next to each other, and the interpreter is opposite them. This would contradict the usual configuration, and the one Rae prefers, where the interpreter is positioned opposite the deaf person but next to or slightly behind the deaf person's interlocutor. I have used this arrangement and find it slightly distracting not to be able to see the interpreter. Melissa, Kali, and Gustav used this setup. Kali and Gustav sat opposite each other, and Melissa sat next to Gustav at a small rectangular table. This caused Kali and Gustav to have to twist sideways when they both needed to see the paper or book they were talking about. The benefit of having the tutor and tutee sit side by side is that they can both look at the paper together and work directly with the English on the page rather than through the interpreter. Of course, the ideal location of the interpreter is whatever the tutee prefers.

Technology

Beginning with *The Practical Tutor* (Meyer and Smith 1987), computers have been considered an option for working with students with sensory and physical disabilities, especially deaf students. Wood (1995) provides a model technique in which a computer is used to type messages back and forth, and Mindess (1999) also mentions this method of communication. I had expected to do observations at a writing center using this technology to communicate with deaf students, but unfortunately I was unable to schedule any observations at that location. The only dyad I observed that used computers extensively was that of Rae and John. They used a computer in all three tutoring sessions I observed, once to review and compose text and twice to do research on the Internet. In all three sessions, communication was facilitated by the interpreter, except when Rae composed text on the computer and John read it, eliminating the need for the interpreter. Rae said in an interview that she preferred this method:

> Because that way he could see how I type my paper, and he could be the observer . . . as opposed to typing the sentences out for me. And so . . . what I prefer to do is to type out the paper and then have him go in and correct the grammar and such. And . . . having him sit there in a different position once we switched, it was better [because] I could just type it out and see what was going on in my mind . . .

and he could easily look over at the screen and make the changes that needed to be made with the grammar, punctuation . . . instead of me telling him what to do . . . it wasn't working out that way.

Tutors and tutees can devise whatever communication methods work best for them. Other promising technologies is computer captioning programs such as CART and C-Print (Stinson and Stuckless 1998). Another technological option is real-time sign language interpretation over the Internet with two-way video and the interpreter in a different location (Osborne 2003).

Miscommunication

Miscommunication between deaf students and hearing tutors occurred most commonly around the intersection of two languages and dissimilar modalities. In a few instances ASL interference occurred, and there were a small number of miscommunications through the interpreter. I have already discussed my belief that ASL influence is not as large a problem in deaf students' writing as folk theories would lead us to believe (Babcock 2006).[7] The most common glitch in communication was a simple request for repetition by the tutee or the interpreter or a statement like "I don't understand." Many times the tutee or the interpreter asked the tutor to repeat something, but this also happened with hearing tutees, although not as frequently.

Although I do not believe ASL interference is as problematic as many people think, it does crop up. The clearest example of possible ASL

---

7. These theories are a naïve application of the contrastive analysis (CA) hypothesis, which has been largely rejected by linguists. Anderson (1993) is the only writer who has explicitly introduced the contrastive analysis hypothesis when discussing deaf students' writing. She did so in a controlled and logical way. In her assessment, CA was "highly subjective; the instructor's assessment of the nature of specific errors was often quite different from the reasons offered by the students for their usage of particular grammatical forms," CA had "very little predictive ability, being most able to forecast errors at the level of phonology and least able to predict errors at the syntactic level," "CA did not account for those errors that derived from language learning strategies rather than from interference," and transfer was "only one strategy used by learners, and not the most important" (73). Indeed, learner errors can be attributed to many other causes.

interference in English I observed came about in an exchange involving Blue, Newby, and Jay, which was mentioned earlier. Blue was working on a paper about her observations on a train, and Newby was reading it with her, making corrections in response to the teacher's comments, when she came upon a tricky sentence:

Newby: Could you sign this sentence for me and have Jay tell me what it says?

Blue: Woman who had the red—Woman who have red hair with ponytail holder, with ponytail holder and green eyes.

Newby: Oh, OK. So, this is—I was a little confused right here. OK . . . Now, "the woman who has."

Blue: [signs, with a closed fist at the back of her head]

Jay: Holds. Ponytail holder.

Newby: . . . So, hold, ponytail holder. You need to tell me what kind of holder it is. OK. This is like [holds book to chest] "she holds the book." This is, right, and that's OK. But you need to—

Jay: I kind of messed it up. She didn't say ponytail holder.

Newby: Right. It's not on there.

Jay: But she did "hold." I probably should have said "hold." That was my interpretation of what she said. I probably should have—

Newby: And this is where . . . she has problems with writing. Because in signing, you can say so much more with fewer words. . . . But on a paper you've gotta write it out. . . . So, I mean this is much more complex and probably harder. . . . So, yeah, signing, it's perfect the way you're doing it. It's just that when you put it on paper . . . I need more to understand.

Blue: I got it. Alright.

Newby: So you need to tell me, and this would be "holder" instead of "holds" with an -s. A ponytail holder. You need to tell me what kind. . . . It's got to have much more stuff than you're used to. Most of us, when we start to write, we probably have to put in more stuff on the paper than when we speak. Just probably if you remember that you need to add more

> to make me see. When you sign, when you sign, she can see it, OK? But in order for me to see it, you've gotta put the words on your paper. OK. Just like learning a foreign language. OK? . . . You're doing great. So you know what to do with that one.

What is interesting about this exchange is that they explicitly discuss the miscommunication, how it happened, and how to correct it. Then Newby discusses the situation and the result, using the problem as a learning opportunity. What Blue had actually written was, "Now, the woman who has a red hair with bow holds and green eyes." Newby assumed that if Blue signed it, then the missing words or unclear meaning would become clear. The problem here is that in writing, Blue had used the word "bow" as the descriptor rather than "ponytail," as Jay interpreted and as Newby expected.

Also, "holds" was written as a verb rather than the expected noun form, "holder," which Jay also supplied. The way Blue signed it, with a closed fist at the back of the head, she was signing "holds" in a different position. The sign HOLDS is usually articulated with a closed fist, palm up, in the signing space in front of the signer, but Blue signed it with a closed fist at the back of the head, representing the position of the ponytail. That this construction was clear to Jay is obvious: she interpreted the word correctly as "ponytail holder." This event could be seen as an instance of ASL interference or of the interpreter's inserting words that were not the deaf tutee's choice. It could also be that Blue did not know the English form "ponytail holder." In either case, ASL interference was sporadic and not highly significant in the data corpus.

I had initially thought that the proper communication mode between deaf tutees and hearing tutors could be determined through research. After doing research and trying to understand the educational needs of deaf people, I have come to realize that the proper communication mode to use in tutoring is whatever the tutee prefers. It is also important to be flexible, not judgmental. For instance, at one potential research site, the assistant director told me that the site rarely used interpreters when tutoring writing with deaf students and preferred computers instead. I immediately thought this was culturally insensitive. Johnson (1996) recommends that writing teachers have occasional conferences with their deaf students without an interpreter present, especially if they need to discuss a problem with the performance of the interpreter. Such discussions could also be of benefit to writing conferences. Tutors and tutees should have an opportunity to meet occasionally without the interpreter present, perhaps to talk about or evaluate the role of the interpreter. Blue and Newby informed me that, from time to time, they had successful conferences without an interpreter and communicated by writing on paper.

Emotion in and around the Tutoring Session

One of my research questions was "What are the participants' feelings surrounding the tutoring session?" I learned about the participants' feelings by observing their words and actions during tutoring sessions and talking about them in interviews. I do not include as displays of affect the slight shifts in interest such as body language and emphasis that were part of the tutoring session. For instance, Kali exclaimed, in response to how many stories Ray Bradbury had written, "He wrote over six hundred of them!" In addition, Rae got excited when she gave her long speech about US relationships with Latin America. Because these types of remarks were directly connected to the content, I did not consider them a display of personal affect. I also do not include remarks that were caught on tape but were unconnected to the tutoring session (e.g., if the tutee and the researcher were joking around before the session began). I concentrate here on explicit remarks that reveal a person's feelings. I also include in this section tutors and tutees relating through encouragement and evaluation, as well as people's reflections on their feelings, both in the tutoring sessions and in the interviews.

Display of Affect

Although I was interested in observing the emotional dimension of tutoring, not all of the participants displayed personal emotion during the tutoring sessions. Perhaps this had to do with gender, as the males in the study showed affect only rarely. In fact, the display of affect was so infrequent that it was difficult to find more than one example in each category. This could mean the categories are unique, the sample was too small, or the categories are actually dimensions rather than subcategories of *display of affect*. Because of the small sample size and the rarity of occurrences, the examples that follow are the only ones that occurred in the study, and the participants mentioned are the only ones who exhibited the behavior in question.

Many times tutors and tutees made positive remarks about their emotional state during the tutoring session. Sometimes these statements would be prompted by a question. At the end of their last tutoring session for the spring 2003 semester, Newby asked Blue whether she had any questions, and Blue responded, "I'll miss you!" with real feeling. The tutees I observed with Newby felt a real affection for her. As mentioned earlier, Newby reflected that, because she is older than the tutees, she has a motherly or even grandmotherly relationship with some of them. Kali expressed positive feelings when Gustav presented her with a large number of handouts. She expressed her gratitude by commenting, "Thank you. I didn't expect this. This is great."

Some remarks showing affect were complex in that they displayed both negative and positive feelings, such as when Blue said to Newby, "It's kind of tough, but I'm just going to try my best," demonstrating effort in the face of difficulty. In addition, in an earlier session she had said, "I'm just trying to do my best. I don't know," mixing motivation and uncertainty. Later, Newby asked Blue, "So, how do you feel about this?" and instead of relating her feelings, Blue answered, "I'm learning, that's all," as if she were resigned to the process. Shareef made few remarks that could be considered displays of affect. Similar to the earlier comments revealing mixed resignation and motivation, Shareef remarked, in response to some corrections he was making, "That's what I'm tryin'a do, man," displaying his effort, frustration, and success. John responded encouragingly, "You know the mistakes you made. That's fine."

At times the tutees made defensive or disparaging remarks or gestures. At one point when Newby asked Blue to repeat a reading passage in her own words, Blue smiled and covered her face as if to say the task was beyond her. When discussing the Janet Jackson presentation,

at times Blue would display worry or uncertainty about her performance. For instance, when Newby remarked, "Something's missing,"
Blue responded with concern: "I did it wrong?" And later in the session,
when Newby pointed out an error, Blue exclaimed, "Maybe . . . I did
the presentation wrong in class yesterday! My goodness!" Sometimes the
tutees made defensive comments. For instance, when Newby told Blue,
"You shouldn't use words if you don't know the meaning of them," Blue
retorted, "But I got a B!" When John suggested to Rae that she eliminate padding, she replied, "I need to have six pages. I was just trying to
add what I could."

Out of frustration, Squirt sometimes made sarcastic comebacks,
asked flippant questions, or made negative comments. For instance,
when talking about her paper, Squirt said, "I just had to type the damn
thing. I was pissed off," recounting her attitude while typing the paper.
She also displayed her frustration in the tutoring session when she
said, "I don't wanna be a writer." I think some of Squirt's seemingly
sarcastic comments and questions were actually genuine responses to
the nondirective techniques Newby was using. For instance, when
Newby asked, "How would these sound if . . . you took these 'ands'
out and made two independent sentences?" and Squirt answered, "I
don't know," perhaps she really did not know or did not understand
that this question was a politely worded suggestion, not an actual
request for information.

Tutors and tutees also displayed affect in body language; for instance,
when Newby became slightly frustrated when Blue did not catch on, she
took off her glasses and sighed. During the tutoring sessions I observed,
Squirt was extremely fidgety, displaying her frustration by touching her
hair, playing with her pencil, and moving around in her chair. When John
and Rae were working on the computer and Rae was telling John what
to enter to search on the Internet and he did not do what she suggested,
she gave a look of annoyance and resignation. When I asked her later
whether she was amused, impatient, or frustrated, she replied:

No, I just felt like, "Oh, man . . ." And he thinks, and he knows better.
And if he does, it's fine. It doesn't really matter to me. I do know
I'm on the Internet all the time. I'm doing a lot of research on the

Internet. So, I feel like *this* is what you should be doing. But like I said today, I'm lazy, I don't feel like getting into anything, I don't feel like blowing up at him or getting emotionally involved. So I just feel like, "Do whatever you want."

John's body language expressed amusement when he asked Rae whether she had the Hacker handbook, showed it, and then smiled as if he were a salesman for the book.

I could not discern a clear pattern for the display of affect besides the fact that females were more likely to verbalize their interior emotional states than males were. Of the tutees who did display affect, there was no clear deaf/hearing split. The two tutees who displayed the most affect were Squirt and Blue, and the only things they had in common was their gender and their tutor, Newby. Since they constituted the only two all-female dyads (all three interpreters were also female), perhaps the female-to-female tutoring relationship is more conducive to displays of affect. I did not observe any other all-female tutoring dyads, so the display of affect could also have to do with Newby as a tutor and the fact that her tutees felt comfortable displaying affect while with her, possibly because of the motherly role that she sometimes assumed with them.

Encouragement and Evaluation

Tutors often offered their tutees encouragement, especially when their confidence was flagging. The tutors' positive evaluations of their work also served as a form of encouragement. In only one case did a tutee evaluate his own progress.

Newby gave encouragement in the form of little pep talks. For instance, she told Blue the following:

And you're not always going to always have someone there to explain it. So you're going to have to work at figuring some of this stuff out. But anytime, you should always ask questions if someone is available to explain it you. So most of us probably learn better with teachers or a tutor helping us to figure out what's on the paper. But we also have to take responsibility and get as much of it as we can. Just keep working at it. It'll get easier. . . . OK? So have you got any questions there?

In an earlier session, Newby had wanted to display how much Blue had learned, so she showed her an earlier paper, which was covered with marks, and compared it to her current paper. When Blue reacted negatively, Newby encouraged her:

Blue: Ah, it's impossible!
Newby: And look at this. Can't you just see? You can see improvement [showing her both papers]. That's improvement. So, you should feel good.
Blue: Yeah.
Newby: And we're all learning as the semester goes on. This is very good. We don't have many marks on this paper *at all*. OK?

Newby also evaluated Blue's work through praise, such as when Blue successfully paraphrased something from the reading:

Blue: You have to be proud, and you have to accept the challenge for yourself.
Newby: Very good. Very good. [motions for Blue to write]

Newby also praised Squirt's work and effort: "That part's gonna be good if you change it that much." Any negative evaluation was phrased delicately, such as "There's some things that you said better in the original paper. Were you in a hurry when you did this?" and "There's some stuff on it we looked at last week that was laid out a little better than what we're looking at now." When Squirt became difficult to work with because of her frustration, Newby evaluated her behavior and said, "You cannot get frustrated and take this attitude of defiance." This was the only time a tutor told a tutee how to behave. As mentioned earlier, Squirt's behavior is most likely related to her frustration due to her learning disability. Since Newby is experienced in special education, she knows how to deal with Squirt's needs in the tutoring session. Moreover, since

Newby is older, she likely felt comfortable directing Squirt's behavior when it was inappropriate.

John often evaluated his tutees' work, both their writing and their efforts during the tutoring sessions. For example, he evaluated Rae's paper as follows: "It's fine right now. For the most part . . . it's good." He evaluated Herrodrick's paper, which he did not actually see, with less enthusiasm: "It's probably OK." Obviously he could not give a whole-heartedly positive evaluation of a paper he had not seen. However, since Herrodrick had already turned the paper in, John might have felt com-pelled to assure him it was all right, much like Newby assured Blue that her presentation was fine even though the written text had some gram-matical errors. John went on to say he was just throwing out ideas as they were discussing what Herrodrick wrote about and assured him it was acceptable if he did not include them:

> You know, these are just . . . questions, [so] if you don't . . . include this in your text, it's not necessarily a bad thing or a good thing. The text is a text. These are just questions that I'm thinking of.

As the discussion continued, John encouraged him again: "So you did tie it back to something concrete. Good," and "It sounds like you're on the right track." He even commended Herrodrick for taking on such a difficult topic and speculated that the teacher would also look favorably on the attempt. John sensed that Herrodrick needed this support since, because of scheduling, he was not able to share the actual paper with the tutor before handing it in. He also encouraged Herrodrick with positive evaluation in their other tutoring sessions.

When John read Shareef's paper, he assessed it positively: "OK. Good. This is good stuff," and when Shareef explained more about what he was doing with the paper, John said, "OK. It's a good idea." John often evaluated Shareef's writing, as he did Herrodrick's, with "Good," "That sounds fine," and "It's a great start." With regard to a detail about using a drumstick for a microphone and some interesting material Shareef had found on a website, he also commented, "That's funny." Often John would say, "Cool," but I think he used this word as a backchannel rather than as an explicit evaluator. For instance, John said, "Cool," where others would say, "Yeah," or "All right."

Similarly to how John evaluated his tutees' work, Gustav evaluated Kali's work with "Very good." Gustav also evaluated her work more specifically, with remarks such as "I really like your word usage. Very colorful language . . . I love this: [reads] 'Celestial destination.' Very, very good . . . Excellent, excellent, excellent. Very good usage here." This praise was spread out over a number of turns, but, of the three tutors I observed, Gustav did offer the most effusive positive evaluation. It is not clear whether the volume and magnitude of praise was because Gustav is an exceptionally enthusiastic tutor or because Kali is a remarkably talented writer. In response to Kali's concern about her poetry interpretation, Gustav reassured her that hers was "as fine an interpretation as any I've ever heard." Gustav is also honest in his evaluation; for instance, he commented on Kali's essay with "It's a little bit too open ended rather than clearly organized."

Tutors also evaluated the tutees' papers in more general terms. In response to Rae's paper John said, "I think you've approached it thoroughly." He also evaluated her paper and her effort by saying "You can definitely expand it to six pages. It shouldn't be a problem." In addition, he asked the tutees to evaluate their own papers. When in a tutoring session with Herrodrick, he invited him to evaluate his own paper: "The paper last time, do you think it came out well?" Newby evaluated Squirt's paper when she said it was not even a C paper and that the draft she had brought the week before was better. Newby did not evaluate any of Blue's papers as a whole, but she did praise her correct use of problematic forms and her improvement in her revisions. Likewise, Gustav's evaluative comments on Kali's paper were more to encourage her process ("So far, so good") than to explicitly assess her product. In another tutoring session, in fact, he commented, "Ah, the paper's very good. In fact, it's written much better than the last one."

The tutees did not evaluate their own papers, but they occasionally reported their teacher's evaluations. For instance, Blue told Newby the following:

[The teacher] read it, and he told me that the paper was good. You know, it had a lot of good descriptions. The only problem with it— he said the paper was good, good description, but I had to write in past tense, present tense.

Squirt also repeated to Newby her teacher's comment that her paper "wasn't good enough" and that she needed to "add more stuff."

The tutees sometimes evaluated the tutors' help and ideas, especially in response to prompting. For instance, at the end of the spring 2003 semester, Newby asked Blue to reflect on their tutoring sessions:

Newby: [I want you to think] about the writing center. How you, what you've learned, maybe how you've come along, how I've helped you. . . . There might be something I might have missed.

Blue: I think that you didn't miss anything. You didn't miss anything. You taught me all this stuff about the verbs, and I've gotten my work done. You've taught me how to do that. You've helped me a lot. I felt fine.

Rae positively evaluated one of John's contributions of a definition of a "banana republic" as a "half-assed republic": "That sums it up. A half-assed republic. I like that. I could use that." Kali evaluated Gustav's contribution about how to organize her paragraphs: "All right. That would be fine. That sounds like a good idea."

The hearing tutees did not explicitly evaluate the tutor or the tutor's contributions during the actual sessions. It is not clear whether Squirt was evaluating the assignment or her paper when, as mentioned earlier, she said, "This is stupid," twice at the end of her tutoring session with Newby. These remarks were probably just another expression of her frustration.

Shareef was the only tutee who evaluated and reflected on his own progress during the tutoring session. When talking about finding his own errors he said this:

I was starting to be able to catch some of the stuff now, catch—the more I do it. You know, catchin' 'em. I think I've probably mastered, got all the mistakes, 'cause I think it's really about learning from your mistakes. . . . Once you learn what you're doing wrong and fix it, I think that's what makes it better.

Shareef is a very active learner and concerned with doing his best.

Reflection

In the interviews, both tutors and tutees reflected on the tutoring sessions, their emotional states, and their evaluation of the proceedings. For instance, Squirt said her conferences with Newby were "awesome" and "fun" and that she liked them. She just wished Newby would "give more tips" and "give me more feedback." Squirt also mentioned that she had tutored a student in her role as a mentor. When I asked Squirt about this experience, she said she primarily offered tips to her tutee. Perhaps because of her learning disability, Squirt prefers direct information to indirect questioning. She also found it frustrating to suspect that Newby had the answers that she needed and withheld them.

Blue stated that she was "pretty motivated to learn how to write. I feel like I'm ready to do it. You know, I feel like I want to learn about verbs and adjectives. I feel pretty inspired to get that information." She also commented that she was grateful to the tutor. In addition, she said she wanted more explanations given to her rather than having to get the answers herself by reading even though her goal is to improve her reading and her vocabulary. In November she said Newby's handout with the verb tenses had helped a lot, although the previous May she had said she did not understand it. Obviously, students will benefit from help only when they are ready for it. In addition, she said she was pleased when the tutor pointed out her errors and helped her make the corrections. In all, she felt good about the tutoring sessions.

Newby stated that she and Squirt "worked quite well together." She also said that she was happy to have had an opportunity to work with Blue. She felt that their discussions had helped her see English differently and that she had "learned an awful lot, and it [did] help me reflect on composition, or formalized writing." She also reflected on how the presence of an observer influenced the tutoring session. She said that at one point she was rushing through the tutoring session because I wanted to interview the tutee afterward. As a seasoned researcher, she was aware that the presence of the camera or the researcher should not have influenced her tutoring.

John stated that he "was a little nervous the first time" he was scheduled to work with Rae because he "didn't know how the dynamic would be. But [he] was surprised that it [was] really similar to a normal session." His nervousness was due to the fact that he "didn't have any history with tutoring deaf or blind students or any students with disabilities. And that's what makes you nervous . . . you feel like, I don't know enough about deaf students." He did not know how he would react if a problem came up, but he indicated that, with the interpreter present, it was much like a regular session. He also commented that he would find it quite difficult, if not impossible, to conduct a tutoring session with a deaf writer without an interpreter. I mentioned the use of writing, either on paper or on a computer, and he said he would have to devise a plan like that. He also reported that no communication problems had arisen in the tutoring sessions. In addition, he mentioned that he felt good and also grateful that he could help Rae. With regard to tutor training, John felt much the same way as Gustav (see the latter's quote at the beginning of chapter 4): one does not learn how to tutor from a book or an article but by doing it.

Rae stated that the tutor she had before John had wasted their time together by questioning her about deafness and her language; on the other hand, she remembered a positive session with a tutor who was an expert signer. She said she was happy with John as a tutor because he was able to work efficiently with the interpreter and was patient with her. She reported that the tutoring went smoothly. I asked Rae about something that I had noticed in the tutoring session. John had printed a great deal of material from the Internet that he felt would help Rae; however, Rae had told him not to because she would not read the material anyway. Then, when John was out of the room, she signed, "Bye-bye trees." She had not directly mentioned the environmental issue to him. She said later in an interview that she would feel comfortable doing that, but she had not actually done so. She had also refrained from saying anything to John about the search terms that he was using on the Internet, which she disagreed with, as discussed earlier. This shows that tutees do not always say what is on their minds; they just go along with what the tutor is doing. I knew Rae had had a negative reaction only because I noticed the expression on her face. John did not.

Outside of college, Herrodrick does his own writing. He is writing a sci-fi/fantasy novel and therefore was surprised that he tested into English Composition I Enhanced with a tutorial component designed for writers who need extra help. However, the tutoring sessions went well, he liked John, and he was inspired to bring his own writing to the tutoring sessions. He said, "John's a great tutor for me." The fact that they shared the same major (film) enabled them to be "basically geared toward the same thing." Herrodrick liked the way John "just sits back and listens to what [he's] saying, which is good." Although he wished John would talk more about philosophy, "he's fulfilling the needs I have during the tutoring sessions." Herrodrick was the only tutee in the study who indicated that the day and time of the tutoring session could be significant. His tutoring session, like Shareef's, was on Friday, which Herrodrick considered his "wind-down day for the week." Having the conference on Friday afternoons allowed him to relax "and basically talk about what actually matters to me. . . . It's about me, then, in the session." Even though he was required to come to tutoring, he said he would continue to come in the future even if he were not required to do so.

Shareef said he loves to write. He is also happy with John as a tutor. He said he needed a guide, and John fulfilled that role. He also said he gained confidence through the tutoring sessions: "I feel like I've stepped up a little bit from where I used to be. I feel like I'm evolving." He liked both John and the tutoring sessions a lot. He also gained a sense of confidence about writing that he did not have before:

> It's been positive. It's a confident feeling. I just feel . . . confident whenever I come to tutoring. And whenever I leave, my confidence go up by a notch every time I come here and I get motivated to do better, you know.

He attributed this rapport to John's being a male student like him; with a female tutor he might have been distracted. Like Herrodrick, he said he would continue the tutoring sessions even when they are no longer required.

On reflection, Kali said that she had had many good tutors and numerous good experiences. When I asked about her attitude toward writing, she replied that she "really . . . enjoy[ed] it a lot . . . . It's like, there's no boundaries. And really, there's no handicap in writing, so I feel that I can write anything." She also explained that she could use more precise words when writing and thus express herself better than when signing. She said she would rather fingerspell than sign so that she could communicate the exact English word that she intended. Her tutoring sessions, she said, were a "very good experience" and gave her "a lot of help." She was satisfied with Gustav's feedback, and she felt that the other tutors she had worked with were quite good as well. She liked receiving handouts.

Kali also mentioned that she is a little shy and did not always ask the tutor to repeat something that she did not understand. She did speak up, however, when she had a tutor who was not working out and asked the director to pair her with someone different. At first, she was nervous about the tutoring sessions because she was shy about having someone read her paper, but then this turned into a feeling of comfort because the tutor had been so helpful. She is more confident now. She also liked making small talk with the tutor before the tutoring session because "It shows they're interested in me as a person, not just a student, you know, another statistic. It makes me more human."

Gustav said he generally felt comfortable working with a deaf student. He remembered that he had felt mildly anxious before working with any student, hearing or deaf, "particularly when a paper is written on a subject that [Gustav is] unfamiliar with." He wants the tutees to get something out of the session, not just to waste an hour of their time. Like Kali, Gustav said that he would like to have a relationship with the student that is more than "a cold and impersonal business experience" and that he likes "the relational aspect of it. . . . That's very pleasant to me." It is interesting that both Kali and Gustav mentioned this, yet they did not talk about anything personal in the two tutoring sessions I observed or the one that was taped for me. Gustav later told me during member checking that he and Kali made small talk during tutoring sessions, just not those that I observed. In his opinion the interpreter was a hindrance to socializing in the tutoring session because Gustav felt that they must get down to business since "there's this other person here." (The same can be said about the presence of the researcher or the tape recorder.) The formal nature of the observation might make tutors and tutees less likely to make small talk, a seeming waste of time.

When I mentioned that some tutors feel guilt when tutoring a deaf student, Gustav strongly denied feeling that way himself. Many tutors, however, do experience this, especially when taking over too much of the editing and proofreading, which goes against their nondirective training (Day 2002). None of the tutors in this study reported feeling guilt for offering what they perceived as too much help in this way. Gustav said that his tutoring style had much to do with his mood, that it was flexible and fluid, and that he had no one way to tutor people since "people have diverse needs." This thought echoes an aphorism of my own, which is "everyone is a special-needs student" since every student has unique needs.

Discourse Features

Quality of talk and interpersonal interactions are important discourse features to note when trying to understand the tutoring process. Discourse analysts have used quality of talk as a way to understand involvement and investment in a conversation. I have classified the interpersonal dimension of talk as those features that contribute not to the actual work of the tutoring session but to the participants' relationships.

Quality of Talk

A variety of salient language features can help us understand what is going on in discourse (Kutz 1997). The two that are relevant to this study are the amount of talk and lexical/pragmatic features.

Amount of Talk

The amount of participant talk shows who controls the conversation (Kutz 1997). Other scholars, however, have found that silence is powerful and may actually indicate control (Nancy Hayward, pers. comm.). On the other hand, in the writing center literature there is general agreement that the tutor should avoid dominating the conversation and should encourage the tutee to talk more and that the one who talks more is probably in control of the exchange. I have decided to use the concept that whoever talks more (takes longer turns) is in control, and if a person gives many minimal, one-word responses, then that person is not controlling the situation. I was not surprised to see that, in general, the tutors talked more than the tutees. This is especially true in the case of deaf students. Newby said that she would like to get Blue to talk (sign) more. Newby is aware that in the tutoring sessions she would ask questions and Blue would often give minimal answers like "Yeah" and "OK." Similarly, with Gustav and Kali, often Gustav would expound on a topic, and Kali would respond with minimal one-word responses like "Right" and "OK." These one-word responses seem more common with the deaf students than the hearing ones. Rae, however, was more in control of the tutoring session than other tutees, including the hearing students. She made a very long remark in the tutorial about her Spanish history paper. It is the longest speech in any of the tutorials I observed. In it she clearly showed that she had learned the class material and internalized it. In a turn of almost a page of transcript, she explained her understanding of imperialism and what the United States has done in Latin America. In the other two sessions I observed with John and Rae, however, John had the longer turns.

Even though Herrodrick and John were equal partners in conversation and their tutoring sessions were collaborative, with each one seeming to contribute equally, John contributed the longest turn in each of their sessions. With Shareef, John also took the longest turns, but the discussion was still collaborative, as they found and fixed errors together. Both John and Shareef used minimal, one-word answers, but these were fairly equally distributed. In Squirt and Newby's tutoring sessions, Newby took the longest turns, but not by much. In many places they went back and forth with very short turns, and as illustrated earlier, most of the dialogue appeared contentious. In the second tutoring session I observed with them, besides when they read aloud from the text, the longest turns consisted of only four typed lines. So, in all of the tutoring sessions except for Rae's of May 8, 2003, the tutor had the longest turns. If length of turn is an indication of control, then the tutors were in control for most of the sessions.

Lexical/Pragmatic Features

Tutors used a variety of pronouns and modals to indicate their relationship to the tutee, the professor, and the subject. John often did this. For instance, when tutoring Rae, he used the conditional when he offered a fix: "I would say . . ." In this way he turned the suggestion back on himself, giving Rae the option of doing what he would do or not. This also reinforced his position as expert, as the apparent assumption behind this construction is that if the tutor would do it this way, then it must be right. However, with Shareef, John used "I would say" not to offer a fix but as a discourse marker or to deflect his comments in general. John also used the conditional in the second person: "You'd break that up" or "You wouldn't . . ." this time deflecting the strength of the suggestion by using the conditional as a polite form.

John also asked Rae whether she "should compare the Castro book with a different book." The use of "should" is more directive, but Rae refused to change books, insisting that her misunderstanding of the book was going to be part of her critique. He also used multiple polite forms like "You'd probably want to . . ." and "I'd like you to maybe expand . . ." At times John was very direct, saying, "You have to" and "You don't have to," but most of the time he used the polite forms. With his hearing tutees, he used similar constructions. With Shareef, however, he was very direct in his comments and used few pronoun or modal features to soften them. He did offer a possible fix to Shareef with "You might say" and then modeled the solution. Perhaps John did not feel the need to soften his comments to Shareef with these discourse features since in those discussions he acted more as an expert on grammar and corrections; thus, as an expert he did not have to soften his comments. In addition, he said, "You need an article there," "You've gotta make it plural," and "You can probably even take it out," which are fairly directive even though they use modals, but in all John did not seem to use as many polite forms with Shareef.

With Herrodrick, the tutoring sessions were a bit different as they focused mostly on ideas. Only at a few points did John use any of these devices. At one point he said, "So, the number one thing you want to do is . . ." and "you would have to," basically framing his advice in the second person with the modal as he did with Rae. He also used the modal "could" ("You could probably extract . . ."), but he used it as a genuine option that he was considering for himself, not as advice for Herrodrick to take. Toward the middle of the second tutoring session I observed with

Herrodrick and John, John recapped what they had done so far: "You could . . . you would be able to . . . you'd probably find . . . You can . . . you might be able to . . .," again not so much as advice but as a summary of what they had talked about and Herrodrick's options from there.

Gustav also used polite forms to deflect the directiveness of his comments. Like John, he used "I would," but he also used the second person (e.g., "You could also change it . . .," "You don't wanna say . . .," "If you wanted to . . . you could . . .," and "you can"). He slipped into the plural "we" a few times, showing shared ownership of the paper: "Here I think we should say . . . ." Some might perceive this as a co-option of the paper, but more likely it displays Gustav's understanding of the collaborative nature of the conference. It really is "we" who do things to the paper in the conference. The passive can also deflect directness, as when Gustav said, "It should be incorporated," since in the passive construction just who is doing the incorporating is left unspecified. Like all of the tutors in the study, Gustav was direct at times with his comments, using the simple imperative: "incorporate this under this point."

Although Newby used nondirective questioning primarily to help her tutees discover what they needed to write, she was fairly direct at times with Blue about what to do to her paper. She used constructions like "You need to add more," "You've got to write more," and "You have to write it." These are directed to the second person and contain directive types of modals ("have to," "got to," "need to"). She also used more conditional constructions like "You could," but she used these when there genuinely was a choice, not as a simple politeness construction. Newby did not use the first person to deflect the directiveness of her comments as often as John and Gustav did, but she did occasionally use a mix of the first and second person with a conditional ("I think you would start a new sentence here") and a mix of the second person and the first person plural ("We could use 'sat' if you took out 'was'").

With Squirt, Newby got her points across mostly through questioning, but she did use some more directive comments with certain constructions that diffused their directiveness. For instance, she used a mix of the first-person plural, the second person, and the directive modal when she said, "We gotta make sense on paper. You've gotta make sense on paper, right?" With this construction she established a rule that we all must follow, and since this logically includes Squirt, she must follow it as well. Other than questions, Newby used some of the directive modals with Squirt, such as "But you've got to figure out for yourself what to do" and "But now you need to work on it." She used the same constructions with both Blue and Squirt except for the use of "could" to indicate a choice; with Squirt she used "could" as a genuine conditional for politeness: "You could sit here and try to recapture . . . ." When correcting Squirt's behavior, at times Newby was very direct: "Stop being difficult," but she also used the first-person plural to politely deflect the behavioral correction: "Come on, Squirt, let's stop that." Squirt was the only tutee for whom the tutor had to explicitly correct behavior.

Interpersonal

Some of the tutoring dyads engaged in discourse of an interpersonal nature, unrelated to the tutoring session. Although I did not observe John and Gustav doing this with their tutees to any extent, they reported that they did so at other times. Perhaps they got to know the tutees early in the semester, before I began observations. Since Newby had particularly close relationships with her tutees, she attempted to connect to them with talk unrelated to the tutoring session. For instance, in the last conference I observed with Newby and Blue, before the session began they engaged in teasing, as Newby asked Blue, "What happened to your hair? . . . Your hair, you didn't comb it, right?" and I joked, "It's beautiful [signing 'beautiful']." Immediately after this exchange and before starting the tutoring session, Newby presented Blue with a book as a gift. This was a display of Newby's commitment to reading and to Blue as a tutee. When Newby told Blue she could stop reading the book and Blue replied that she was not finished yet, Newby evaluated her effort: "OK. Good. Good, good. Great."

On other occasions, Newby encouraged Blue to read, aside from the tutoring session or her schoolwork, by recommending books and other materials to her. For instance, she suggested that Blue read one of the books by deaf actress Marlee Matlin. She also encouraged Blue in her acting by suggesting she get involved with Deaf theater. Perhaps Newby, as a woman, was more likely to relate to her tutees on a personal level than were Gustav and John. Shareef ended one of the tutoring sessions with a humorous comment, directed at his awareness of the camera and being recorded. He played an announcer and said, "That concludes our time writing. I hope you enjoyed it."

Personal Qualities

In interviews, I asked the participants what qualities they looked for in a tutor and a tutee. In this section, the interviews with the administrators become relevant since they are the ones who hire, train, and decide which tutors will be working with deaf students. I also asked the tutors and tutees for their opinions about the characteristics they possessed or thought were ideal or ineffective.

Student Characteristics

John characterized Rae as an ideal tutee because she took charge in the session and knew what she wanted to work on. Speaking of tutees in general, he said that many students have trouble putting their thoughts into writing and that, although students' needs vary, the tutoring process is the same.

Newby discussed motivation and maturity as important characteristics for a tutee. She has a good deal of respect for Blue and how well her education has progressed despite the obstacles she has encountered as a deaf black girl from the inner city. Newby also thinks Blue is not overly familiar with written language and thus needs to read more to familiarize herself with the conventions of writing. She thinks that many inner-city students experience a cultural mismatch between their home and school cultures and that students need to be "acclimated to the [school] culture." She also stated that she works with "individual students differently." At Davis, many of the students are artists, so she mentioned that as artists they think creatively, not linearly.

Gustav stated that Kali was extremely motivated. He also mentioned another tutee, an ESL student, who was also motivated and brilliant. Because he apparently looks at each tutee as an individual, he did not characterize them in general. He agreed with his supervisor's assessment of Kali, which is that she is a different type of student as she is quite motivated and a very good student, not the "typical community college student." He also implied that she was on a higher level than some of his other students. In addition, he characterized the ideal tutee as being "completely in control. If the student ever comes to the tutoring session, they will have an assignment which they are working on. And generally [Kali] brings in something. Sometimes one paper from one class, sometimes two." Gustav makes it clear that he does not group people by their disabilities, that people can have any traits or attributes whatsoever, and that these are not necessarily linked to their disability.

Ann, the director of the Davis College writing center, characterized the roles of the tutor and tutee as mutual and reciprocal: "I don't think it's ever as student centered to where the student is running it. You know, whipping the tutor into shape or anything like that. But that there's a nice dynamic, you know, of support and trust."

Brock is the assistant director of the Davis College Writing Center. He did not speak about student characteristics per se but mentioned a blind student who ended up teaching the tutor about computers. So, the instruction and expertise can go both ways. He called it "comfort and two-way teaching." It is interesting that Ann and Brock both talked about tutoring as a collaborative endeavor. This attitude reflects the values they hold about tutoring and the tutoring culture at their particular writing center.

Daisy is the disabilities services coordinator at Stanhope College. She remarked that both tutors and tutees have to be aware of their personal learning styles. She also said that tutees may be embarrassed about not understanding things and sometimes say, "Yes, I understand," when they really do not. (Blue told me she did this with the handout on verbs.) Kali also mentioned not necessarily telling the tutor when she did not understand something. Daisy stressed that the tutees need to feel comfortable enough to ask questions or request further explanations if they do not understand.

Referring to student characteristics, Ted, the director of the Academic Success Center at Stanhope College, recommends that deaf students be treated like any other student. Specifically he mentioned that they will be just as grateful as any other student for the tutoring help. Reflecting on his experience tutoring Kali, he said she was a very hard worker and quite enjoyable to work with: "You could tell that she wanted to learn, and she was definitely putting in the time. She would come in with essays that she was writing on her own just because she wanted to stay ahead and wanted to practice." Clearly Kali is a motivated student.

Tutor Characteristics

The tutees, tutors, and administrators all talked about the qualities of an ideal tutor, both in general and specifically for deaf students. Rae told me about an ineffective tutor who had wasted her time with irrelevant questions and was insensitive to her goals for the tutoring session. From this we can interpolate that a tutor who works with deaf students should ask only relevant questions and be sensitive to tutees' needs. Rae appreciated the abundant advice that John gave her during their sessions. She also added patience, understanding, rapport, clarity of explanations, and accommodation to the wants of the tutee as positive tutor qualities. In addition, she reported a very positive tutoring experience with a tutor who was fluent in ASL and thus considers sign language a desirable skill in a tutor.

Squirt wanted a tutor to give tips and explain things. She mentioned that she had seen numerous tutors at the writing center and that "it was all positive. I really liked it." She appreciated the help and support the tutors gave her, as well as the ideas they suggested. She said Newby "explain[ed] stuff. I just like her to explain things more." She wanted Newby to give her more feedback. In all, she said the tutoring sessions were "awesome" and "fun."

Newby said that important tutor characteristics are being student centered, being able to determine students' needs, and having empathy and rapport with the students. She also said she is careful to introduce topics only when students are ready: "You have to meet the students where they are." John reflected that it is not so much training that makes a tutor: tutoring is more instinctual. He values explanation and thoroughness in his tutoring, and, like the others, he feels that one tutors each student differently. Gustav also made the comment that opens chapter 4, that tutoring is not something that one can learn about in an article—one has to experience it. So, a good quality for a tutor is to be able to learn by doing. He also stressed treating all students as individuals.

Brock talked about tutor qualities such as patience, understanding, and knowledge of ASL. This last item can be controversial, as other students whose native language is not English are not usually tutored in their native language; moreover, Wood (1995) has reported that her deaf students did not progress quickly when tutored in ASL. Nonetheless, Brock explained that having a tutor who knew ASL helped the Davis Writing Center's relationship with the Deaf community:

> Brock: We did used to have a writing consultant . . . . in [the] ASL department. . . . He was a superstar and worked very hard, and that was nice to have, somebody who could speak with students directly . . .
>
> Rebecca: You told me there was a while ago a tutor here who was fluent in sign language.
>
> Brock: Extremely fluent.
>
> Rebecca: And that attracted more deaf people to the writing center?
>
> Brock: Yes. In fact, at one time we had four students, [student A], [student B], and actually two other people: [student B's] friends. . . . Ah, yeah, so there were four students, and they were all seeing [the tutor]. You know, the word got out: There's this guy, and you don't even need an interpreter, you can just sign up whenever; you don't have to worry about arranging an interpreter . . . 'cause I did find that when we had that person on staff . . . It might have been that these students were all just coming here at the same time, too, but I can't predict that that's necessarily why it happened, but we did have more of a turnout from the hearing-impaired community.

Although Wood (1995) has said that deaf students did not progress as quickly with a tutor who used sign language, she offered no research to back up that statement. It seems that the good relationship with the Deaf community that can be built by having a tutor who knows sign language outweighs any possible, although unproven, educational setbacks. In addition, schools like Gallaudet University and Harper College in Palentine, Illinois, which serves deaf and hard of hearing students through the Kimball Hill Family Deaf Institute, use tutors who know sign language, and people interested in serving deaf students would probably do well to follow or at least investigate their example.

Ann mentioned the following qualities as important for a tutor who will be working with deaf students: good interpersonal skills, a capable tutor in "regular criteria," personality, tolerance, and willingness to tutor these students. Also, she said someone whom students might respond to well would make a good tutor for deaf tutees. I was unable to learn what the "regular criteria" and the personality of such a tutor would be, but the Davis College tutor handbook stresses the satisfaction tutors get from helping others, the enhancement of their own learning that comes from tutoring, and the enjoyment of working with other tutors and tutees.

Daisy, the disabilities services coordinator at Stanhope, said that tutees gave her feedback on the school's tutors. The positive feedback was about help and understanding, and the negative feedback mentioned lack of explanation and understanding. She said tutors have to be aware of certain things (e.g., deaf students might not have sufficient vocabulary to talk about the subject matter). Both Rae and Blue mentioned lack of vocabulary as a problem. Daisy also said that tutors of deaf students should be open minded and "willing to try something different with a different kind of student." She also mentioned encouragement and caring. Most important, tutors need to be able to adapt their teaching method to the student's learning style, which requires flexibility. She also recommended that tutors not only give explanations but also show examples to deaf students and encourage them to ask questions if they do not understand something.

Ted is the only administrator in the study who has actually tutored one of the deaf participants, so he brings a unique perspective to this discussion. When looking for desirable qualities in a tutor for a deaf student, he takes into account the feedback that the students have given Daisy, who works closely with him. Another positive aspect at Stanhope is that the administrators and staff are very open and the tutors do not have a problem working with anyone with a disability. Perhaps this is because all of Stanhope's tutors are professional, degreed tutors. Ted said his tutors are comfortable working with anyone, and in turn the students feel comfortable with the tutors. He linked his tutors' confidence, professionalism, and ability to deal with all kinds of students to their professional status.

Culture

I had expected to find more cultural factors affecting tutoring than were evident in the data. For instance, I anticipated finding that tutoring sessions with deaf writers would take more time for cultural reasons, but since the appointments were fairly regimented at the sites I visited, I did not see time as a factor. With a weekly session the tutoring could always continue the next week. I did observe a tutoring session where time was a factor; this was the session that was conducted entirely in writing with the deaf writer who declined further observation. He and his tutor communicated by handwritten notes, which was very time consuming: The session lasted more than seventy-five minutes. Barnes (2006) states that time constraints were a common theme throughout the work of the deaf students and tutors whom she studied.

Tutors should be knowledgeable about the language and culture of the Deaf community (Lane 1992). Newby began sign language classes and got involved in researching Deaf culture. Gustav knows some sign language but does not use it with Kali. John feels that as long as the interpreter is there, he does not need to be familiar with sign language and Deaf culture.

The following exchange illustrates the cultural and physical factors relating to deafness that can affect tutoring. Blue had used a word from a source but did not know its meaning, and Newby attempted to have Blue put the word in question into her own words. The problem was that the content of the passage was outside Blue's cultural and physical knowledge (see the full exchange on p. 49).

> Newby: [turns the page, reads] Do you know this word? ["culled"]
> Blue: No. I just got it on the Internet. [laughs]
> Newby: You shouldn't use words if you don't know the meaning of them.

Blue: But I got a B!

Newby: What do you think it means from what the sentence says?

Blue: Maybe like she's a hard worker?

Newby: [takes pen, points to paper] What does she do here? Just tell me. This sentence, when you say "she culled from one album seven top-five singles. What does it mean that she "culled"? In your own words, how would you say that?

Deaf young people do not listen to popular music in the same way hearing young people do. Because Blue does not relate to music in this way, she finds it extremely hard to understand the concept of a "top-five single." From her responses it is clear that she primarily relates to Janet Jackson as a dancer, an actress, and a hard worker. Blue cannot understand not only the task that Newby has set up for her but also the concepts they are discussing, as songs, top-five singles, and albums are probably not a part of her deaf reality.

Thus, tutors should keep cultural and physical factors in mind when tutoring deaf students. Take, for example, this exchange between Newby and Blue about Janet Jackson. It may be quite difficult for a deaf student to comprehend a hearing experience such as listening to music and related topics, such as top-five singles. Perhaps in this case the tutor or interpreter could have intervened and explained what a top-five single was. Also, when Blue insisted on describing Janet Jackson as a dancer and a hard worker, the tutor could have discussed how hearing people consider Janet Jackson as primarily a singer. Newby got close to this when she said, "We're not talking about dancing, we're talking about singing." Blue's view of Jackson as primarily a dancer could be more a result of Blue's interest in dancing than of her deafness.

However, most deaf people do not have enough hearing to listen to and enjoy music the same way hearing people do. Deaf teenagers may be unaware of current trends in popular music, something that strongly separates them from their hearing peers (Johnson 1996). This is just one example of a cultural factor, but I invite the reader to imagine similar situations in the classroom or the writing center, where teachers and tutors assume people can hear, and the effects of those assumptions on deaf people. Johnson also discusses several common writing assignments that are biased against deaf students, such as an activity that asks students to imagine they cannot hear and then reflect on the experience. How is a deaf person to relate to this activity? For one, it implies that deaf students are not considered as a possible audience for the assignment.

Another cultural factor is language. Ideally, all hearing people should know some form of sign language, but this is especially the case for tutors who will be working with deaf students. These individuals should know some ASL (fingerspelling at a minimum) and be somewhat familiar with signed languages and Deaf culture. I had also expected that tutors and tutees would feel frustrated with hands-off (Chappell 1982) and non-directive tutoring techniques because of the value deaf people place on "straight talk" (Mindess 1999).

The nondirective technique was also problematic for Squirt, a hearing student with a learning disability. Gustav used a fairly directive technique, and his tutoring method was well received by Kali: a minimum of miscommunication took place during the sessions I observed. I had also expected to find that deaf students' loquacity would prove exasperating for tutors who expected fairly short answers to their questions. What I actually found was that the deaf tutees gave many minimal, one-word answers like "Yeah" and "OK" and only rarely took long turns.

Tutoring Techniques and Learner Characteristics

Sometimes tutoring techniques and learner characteristics can conflict. For Squirt, a student with a learning disability, some of the nondirective tutoring techniques that Newby used proved frustrating. In addition, her seemingly smart-alecky answers could be a true misunderstanding of the illocutionary force of an utterance. Learners occasionally have trouble understanding that, in the classroom, sometimes a question can actually be a command (Campbell 1986). Although Campbell's research was based in the classroom, the concepts clearly apply to the tutoring context as well. Squirt's learning disability can result in the same type of mismatch between the speaker's intention and the hearer's perception. According to Squirt's mother, a former teacher, Squirt has receptive and expressive language deficits. These impede her ability to read and express herself orally in a clear, concise, grammatically correct manner. She has difficulty decoding nuances of social language. . . . She is certainly open to the path of least resistance, which leads to frustration when required to work through an assignment rather than be given the answer by the person helping her. I found this to be common with LD students in my classes. There is often a need to know that they are on the right track and [they] lack confidence in their own ability. I think this may also be somewhat true for Squirt. (email, June 23, 2004)

Although Squirt was vexed by some of Newby's techniques, it was important that she work through "what [she] need[ed] to do to write the paper" herself.

Squirt's annoyance is evident in the following exchange:

Newby: Well, how do you know that your other stuff wasn't good?
Squirt: I don't know.
Newby: Come on, Squirt.
Squirt: I don't know. If you want to know, then why don't you ask [the teacher]?

Although I thought at first that Squirt was being rude or ornery, she later told me in an interview that she was simply irritated. Her aggravation with the assignment was compounded by her impatience with Newby's nondirective tutoring technique. Squirt wanted to be given answers, not to be asked questions. In one session, Squirt answered, "I don't know" to Newby's questions twenty-eight times. I am sure she often knew the answer, but her response to the nondirective technique was to simply say, "I don't know." Newby and Squirt also engaged in metadiscourse about the situation:

Squirt: So, tell me what to take out, and just tell me what to do, and I'll do it.
Newby: But you've got to figure out for yourself what to do.
Squirt: I know. I know.
Newby: But that's why—
Squirt: That's why you're the tutor. You're supposed to—

Newby: Am I not helping you?

Squirt: Not much.

Newby: Not much? I mean, what is it that I can do to help you?

Squirt: I don't know.

. . .

Newby: So, now, if you—OK. You say that the story is a journey of David's life.

Squirt: Right.

Newby: And how it was an attempt for him to come to terms with who he was and what his sexual orientation really was.

Squirt: Yeah. Right.

Newby: OK. So, when you tell me that, you've got to go through and find instances that support this.

Squirt: So how can I do that?

When Newby gives Squirt information, she is happy, and she can follow. Questions clearly irritate her. Newby reflected in an interview that even though Squirt is gay, she found it difficult to discuss the issue of coming out in her papers and tutoring sessions: "Squirt is gay, but she doesn't like to write about it." As mentioned earlier, however, Squirt told me that Newby's analysis of the situation is incorrect. In the tutoring session, when Newby asked Squirt why it was difficult for her to write this paper, she replied, "I don't know. It's just weird. I don't know. I don't know. I just want to get this done and over with." Because Squirt often reads for pleasure, it is not that she does not like to read. In an interview with me she said she liked the books she was reading for the course, and she liked writing, but the hardest thing about writing the paper on *Giovanni's Room* was organization. Newby's questions simply confused her because she desired direction and explanation.

Interpersonal issues are important for all of the tutoring sessions, not just those between hearing tutors and deaf tutees. The issue of affect and gender is also one that would be worthwhile to explore further. Actually, the differences between tutoring dyads of different gender matchups were the most significant differences of the study. But what does it matter that certain tutoring dyads are more likely to show affect? Is affect important, and if it is, do males need to be encouraged to be more demonstrative?

⌒

Administrators

The descriptions of the administrators are not as rich as those of the tutors, tutees, and interpreters. I did not interact with them as extensively as I did with the other participants.

Brock

Brock is the assistant writing center director at Davis College. He is somewhere between twenty-five and thirty-five, white, and hearing. He is extremely involved in the writing center community and often takes groups of tutors to the National Conference on Peer Tutoring in Writing. He enjoys directing the writing center and also teaches English at the college. He was Herrodrick's writing teacher during the course of the study. Brock is the only participant I knew before beginning the study.

When assigning tutors to work with students who have disabilities, Brock tends to place them with one of those who specialize in ESL or learning disabilities if that is appropriate. If their schedules are already booked, his next step is to look at "who's been here longer, who's got the most experiences, say, from an instructor who might have dealt with students in that realm, who do we think is more gentle or understanding and patient?" Like so many others in the study, Brock said the ideal tutor for a deaf person would be one who knows sign language, and he said he had once employed a tutor who possessed this skill.

Ann and Brock share the teaching responsibility for the tutor-training class. They do not specifically touch on students with disabilities, but they discuss "learning differences." Brock said he would like to, but they have very few students with disabilities who come into the writing center. In a future semester he has plans to "eventually move in that direction" with "a whole class dedicated to working with students with special circumstances." He said that part of the problem was that the tutors felt that they needed work on English grammar to be able to discuss the issues that arise in the tutoring sessions, and this grammar review took up much of the time dedicated to training.

As for his definition of a successful tutoring session, Brock believes that "both the student and the consultant walk away from the session feeling that they learned something" and explained that they believe in "two-way teaching":

> If the consultant walks away feeling that they spent the whole time teaching . . . that's not our mission . . . in tutoring . . . I also think that one of the big considerations for . . . an effective tutoring session would be that both walked away comfortable or while they were in the session felt comfortable. They might have felt discomfort with . . . the actual subject matter. There might be discomfort with the fact that this paper has to be rewritten, but overall they feel comfortable to feel this discomfort with someone else. . . . There has to be some sort of level of acceptance where . . . difficult things can be discussed sometimes. . . . The comfort and the two-way teaching are . . . what I stress over and over again.

Ann

Ann, a middle-aged white woman, is the director of the writing center at Davis College. She is extremely nice and accommodating. She was also very interested in my research topic, and we spoke at length about the issues involved. She thought deeply about the research questions I posed and was inspired to rethink her tutor-training class with regard to including information on students with disabilities. In addition to being the director of the writing center, she also teaches English at the college. Her former husband was hard of hearing, and she has also had a personal experience with hearing loss.

Ann believes that a successful session is one in which

> the student is able to get their needs met. And if they didn't know what those needs were, [then] the tutor would somehow help to determine [them]. I call us a student-centered center, and that's a big part of what that means. The students . . . feel that it's their session and that they can get out of it what they need. That doesn't always happen, and it doesn't always happen right away. [Sometimes] they see their tutor as an authority figure, and they come in and say, "Fix my paper" . . . so it really depends on the individual.

Ann went on to explain how the students need to be "aware that it's their session" and that they can use the session to "improve their writing . . . because they don't know at first. A lot of them just don't know [how to lead the session or talk about writing] . . . and that's a big part of tutoring, steering, or guiding, or coaching, sometimes."

Before working with me on this study, Ann had not given much thought to tutors working with deaf students. She assumed, like many do, that the presence of an interpreter was all that was needed and would make the session the same as the others. She also thinks, like so many people, that "the ideal way to [tutor deaf students] would be if the tutor knew sign language." When she assigns tutors to students, she tries to "keep the lines of communication open" to make sure everyone is comfortable and benefiting from the session, and "if the dynamic didn't work, we would change it immediately." Talking about the work they do with deaf students, she said that "it seems we had . . . a level of satisfaction from the students . . . and . . . the tutors who tutored them . . . are usually surprised that it wasn't as difficult as they thought. . . . [They] actually end up getting excited about it sometimes. . . . I guess until someone says, 'This is absolutely the best thing to do,' I'll just continue doing what we're doing."

Ted

Ted, who is in his thirties, white, and hearing, is the director of the Stanhope College Academic Assistance Center. His background is in writing and English. He is also the only administrator to tutor a deaf student; in a previous semester he tutored study participant Kali. He hires only professional tutors, and their training consists of watching a series of videos, shadowing an expert tutor, and attending an all-day, in-service workshop once per semester.

When I asked Ted about the strengths of his program, he answered, "I think we have a good staff who doesn't have any problem sitting down with anybody and conveying subject matter. I've never had anybody approach me and say, 'I have trouble working with this person' because of any disability. . . . I think everybody's pretty open to helping whoever comes in the door . . . and I think that [the tutors] make people feel very comfortable." He said his tutors try to learn a few words of sign language just to make deaf students feel comfortable. Like most other participants and administrators, he mentioned that he would like to hire a tutor who knew sign language to work with deaf clients.

The disabilities services coordinator helps schedule the tutoring sessions for students with disabilities, and she considers the students' feedback when suggesting tutors for them to work with. He would like to welcome even more students with disabilities to the learning center, especially deaf students: "I know there's a lot more out there that could use our assistance."

His advice for those who will be tutoring a deaf student is "that [deaf students are] just students like everybody else. It's not important that their means of communication is a bit different. They're just a student who needs help, and your job is to give them that help." His definition of an effective tutoring session is one that "give[s] people the skills they need to be effective students independently of us."

Specific techniques that he uses when tutoring a deaf student are frequent checks to see whether the student understands the material. When I asked him about working with Kali in particular, he answered, "I enjoy it. And as I said, I approach it just like any other tutoring session. . . . Kali's so fun to work with that I'm biased in a good way. . . .

She was a hard worker. You could tell that she wanted to learn, and she was definitely putting in the time. She would come in with essays that she was writing on her own just because she wanted to stay ahead and practice."

Daisy

Daisy, who is in her forties, white, and hearing, is the director of Disabilities Services at Stanhope. She also teaches ASL at the college and is familiar with cross-cultural issues between the Deaf and hearing cultures. We spoke at length about the concerns surrounding disability and the tutoring session.

Daisy sometimes teaches tutors about disabilities. Part of this instruction involves a learning-styles questionnaire for both the tutors and the students. She explains that "everyone has their teaching styles and their learning styles." She provides tutors with "a lot of tips" on working with the various approaches to learning. She also talks about "emotionally [and] psychologically supporting students. And where students might be coming from. . . . Some students might come from a long history of failures. Sometimes that in itself—the lack of self-confidence, poor self-image—does a lot to their inabilities to grab onto the material. Sometimes you can boost that self-confidence. . . . It makes a difference."

In order to ensure that the tutoring sessions are successful, she solicits feedback from all of the participants. What she suggests might happen is very different from what Linda told me takes place at Davis. Although Daisy mentioned the code of ethics, she described the following:

> Sometimes [the interpreter] can actually pinpoint why a student isn't getting something. And sometimes it's that the tutor isn't recognizing [that] a student doesn't get it. So, we kind of have a little system in place. . . . . If . . . the student doesn't get it [the first] couple of times, by then the student's ready to just go, "Yeah. I get it." Because [the student is] too embarrassed to say another time, "I'm still confused." But . . . if the interpreter recognizes, "Oh, this student still doesn't get this," [the interpreter can] . . . say to the student, "You know, why

don't you explain to the tutor how to do that?" . . . or "Why don't you explain to the tutor how you would write the next paragraph or what changes you would make in the next paragraph?" So the tutor can actually see [the student is] not getting it. Or [the student] still [doesn't] know how to do it. And sometimes the student actually thinks that they understand, [but] they don't.

Regarding the code of ethics, she explained as follows:

> In education there's a little bit of . . . leeway. And if it's blatantly clear to us that this student is still very lost, [the interpreter will] sometimes say, "Can you explain to the tutor, you know, how you do the next paragraph . . . ?" And then the tutor will go, "Oh yeah. Show me that." You know, they'll kind of work together. And that's our clue to them that we think the student still might not get this. And a lot of times students will just say, "Now, they're really nice to me, and they['re] really try[ing] to help me understand, but I'm still not getting it" . . . and sometimes [the student might think], "I don't want [the tutor] to think I'm not smart or I'm stupid." You know. So we do impress on a lot of students [that they can and actually *should* ask the tutor], "Can you explain it a different way? I [still] didn't understand."

Daisy also meets with the tutors and interpreters to discuss the sessions when they feel frustrated or do not know how to get through to a student: "Sometimes the interpreter will have a suggestion that we can pass back. I'll have the interpreter . . . meet with us." So Daisy and the interpreter will offer some ideas to the tutors, who are usually quite eager to learn new strategies.

As mentioned earlier, Daisy told me that her criteria for a tutor who can work effectively with deaf students would be "someone who's open minded, willing to try new things." A tutor whose attitude was "This is how I tutor, this is how I teach, and that's that" would likely be unsuccessful. She feels that "if you don't have someone who's willing to try something different with a different kind of student or . . . to be encouraging and caring about the student being successful, it's not gonna work.

So, they may almost have to change their teaching style at times. . . . . If they have a student that's very visual, like most of our deaf students, [who need to] see [the material] on the paper, [and the tutor] tend[s] to be an auditory teacher, it's . . . never going to work." Daisy explained further: "You can lecture all day, but if your student is visual, if you don't write examples and show [them] on the paper, [the deaf students are] not ever gonna get it." Daisy thinks that a good tutor would be willing to use the necessary techniques and be open to ideas and suggestions.

Her definition of an effective tutoring session is one in which "the tutor works along with the interpreter, who also works along with the student and the tutor. That's the real key, that the three of them work well together. And . . . the students feel open enough to be able to ask questions, and . . . the tutor invites that . . . and says, 'I want you to tell me if you don't understand. I want to explain another way.'" Daisy feels that an important aspect is for the tutor and the tutee to be "able to communicate, the students feeling very free to ask questions."

Sometimes Daisy suggests that the tutor, to check understanding, ask the student to show an example of what the two of them have been talking about. She feels tutors should "always be very positive and just have that openness so the student can feel good about saying, 'I got it [or] I didn't get it.'" Daisy also recommends that tutors say to their tutees, "If I'm not explaining it in a good way, tell me so I can try another way." She believes that if the tutees "don't feel that openness, and they don't feel they can ask questions, they're never gonna learn from [the tutor]. And if the tutor's not willing to change their style and [is] not even teaching in the style the student wants, the student can't learn." Daisy believes that open communication and the match between teaching and learning styles are the most important aspects of successfully tutoring a deaf student or any student with a disability.

CHAPTER 6

⌐∼⌐

Tutoring Deaf Students in the Writing Center

THE OVERARCHING PURPOSE of the research reported in this volume was to discover how tutoring sessions between a deaf tutee and a hearing tutor are conducted. As I analyzed the data, I looked at the dynamic between the participants, what was taught and learned, what information was expressed and how it was conveyed, what specific tutoring practices were used, how the participants felt, and what other factors (e.g., communication) influenced the session. The formal research questions were as follows:

- What is the content of a tutorial involving a deaf tutee and a hearing tutor, and is it different from the material that is covered when the participants are a hearing tutor and a hearing student?
- How does the tutoring take place? What are the participants' roles and behaviors? What techniques are used?
- What are the contributing and complicating factors: communication, affect, others?

In all, tutoring deaf students and hearing students is not that different. Both types of students want to improve their written compositions and their reading, writing, and research skills. The main differences are communication mode and certain foci of content and practice. With a deaf student, the tutoring session appears more likely to be focused on reading for understanding or editing and proofreading, with special attention to grammar. Other key differences seem to be the appropriateness of the directiveness factor and whether hearing and having an "ear" for the language is stressed. In tutorials with deaf students, learning rules of grammar rather than what "sounds right" appears to be stressed. In this conclusion, the interpreters emerge as the star of the tutoring session, and their words become the most important voices, both literally and figuratively. It is the interpreters' job to translate both language and culture, and in turn, they have helped me unravel what was going on in the sessions. Indeed, the interpreter may be the most important factor in the tutoring equation, as the type of tutoring session I describe here could not take place without an interpreter.

Relevant Factors in Tutoring

After phrasing one of the initial research questions with the word "dynamic," I thought nothing of it until the analysis stage. When I tried to look up "dynamic" in my dictionary to see just what I meant by the term, I saw that, as an adjective, it has to do with energy and force, and "dynamics" as a noun has to do with "various forces, physical and moral, operating in any field" (Guralnik 1964, 234). So, what do the energy and force surrounding the tutoring session comprise? What are the physical and moral factors involved in tutoring? The energy and force are mostly positive, and they are geared toward gaining the necessary and desired literacy skills. In addition, all of the student participants share the positive energy of motivation. The *physical* factors are the placement of bodies, the environment, the ambient temperature, people's clothes, textual materials like papers and books, technology, demographic factors, the mode of communication, and visual, aural, and tactile stimuli. The *moral* factors are evaluative questions such as what is good tutoring? What are the qualities of a good tutor? A good tutee? Most of the respondents valued the tutor as someone who will help, give advice and suggestions as needed, and be sensitive to the needs of the tutee.

The first research question dealt with the content of the tutoring session between a deaf student and a hearing tutor. The content or focus of all of the sessions I observed, with both deaf and hearing tutees, consisted either of writing or information work. All of the tutees in the study worked on literacy—reading and writing—to some extent. They worked on planning, composing, revising, editing, and reflecting on what they wrote. The participants' effort centered on generating ideas for writing assignments, actual composing, revising (either locally or globally), and reflecting on what was written.

The tutees also worked on reading and research, which was somewhat of a surprise. This activity consisted of gathering and understanding information. An example of understanding information is working on reading comprehension, and an example of gathering information is doing research. I observed both deaf and hearing tutees engaging in all of these activities, and all of the tutees also revised for lower-order concerns. Of the white hearing tutees, Squirt and Herrodrick, this attention to LOCs was minimal; the deaf students as a whole, however, spent more time editing and proofreading than the hearing students, with the exception of Shareef, the one hearing student who spoke a nonstandard dialect. All of the deaf tutees worked extensively, if not exclusively, on mechanical correctness in their written products.

The only hearing tutee who worked on reading and understanding texts was Squirt, who also was the only tutee in the study who was taking a literature class. One interesting pattern I noticed was that local revision was being done more with nonmainstream students, such as urban students, nontraditional students, and black students, whereas work on ideas was more common with white suburban students, regardless of hearing status. Nevertheless, the current study sample is too small to make any generalizations, and I offer this only as an observation or a possible avenue for further research. Most interestingly for this study, all of the deaf tutees worked on reading and understanding written texts.

At the Davis College writing center, tutors are trained to follow a hierarchy of error (see chapter 4), whereas the Davis College tutor handbook remarks that "indeed, there may be some sessions spent entirely on grammar," and "Consultants . . . may even find situations that call for working on cosmetic concerns first (or even simultaneously with global concerns)."

Consultants at Davis also read articles (Powers 1993; Neff 1994) that challenge nondirectivity and no editing/proofreading policies for certain students. At Stanhope, according to Gustav, tutors are "warned not to be a proofreading service. . . . You don't want a student to just come in and you just correct their mistakes and don't tell them what the mistakes are or give them any direction to . . . avoid those mistakes in the future." Because of the tutors' training and the results of an earlier study (Day 2002), I anticipated that the tutors would feel uncomfortable with editing and proofreading.

Although it seems counter to writing center dogma, deaf students may be in a unique position to qualify for special help in correcting their papers. This concept of offering editing and proofreading help of the "fix-it-shop" variety seems to rub many writing center people the wrong way. But why should it? The anti-fix-it-shop concept harkens back to North (1984a) and ultimately to the fear of early writing centers that they would be seen as remedial and therefore low in status (Grimm 1999; Carino 2003; Clark and Healy 1996). The truth is that some writers need help in editing and proofreading, and not all them want a long, drawn-out grammatical explanation of every error. Interpreter Linda wonders "how much learning can actually happen for someone in their twenties who is coming to college who just really wants to turn in a paper." She explained her attitude:

> I could come into a tutoring session myself and say, "I know I have grammatical errors or structural errors," for example, and say, "I don't need to know what the rule is called. It's not important to me 'cause I'm not going to remember it after today's tutoring session. Just tell me . . . how to fix what I did wrong." That's me. And I would imagine a lot of people feel that way.

Powers (1993) suggests that ESL writers may need more direction, and I think this is also true for deaf writers. Of course, the tutor should offer an explanation and be ready to give it if needed, but this should be the tutee's preference, especially the deaf tutees, who are in a unique linguistic situation. Interpreter Jay said that many of the tutoring sessions she interpreted focused mainly on grammar and course content. She said sometimes a whole hour would be taken up discussing one grammatical concept. For instance, Newby and Blue spent an entire tutoring session correcting verb tenses in Blue's paper. Tutors should beware of focusing too much on correctness and not enough on content.

It is easy to say that all of the students want the tutor to fix their papers for them, but in this study, both deaf and hearing students said that they wanted to learn to correct their own errors and found satisfaction in that. So, there is a tension between wanting the tutor to correct the paper and wanting the knowledge and skill to correct one's own paper. Editing and grammatical corrections were accomplished through directive, non-directive, and collaborative techniques. Also, all of the tutors shared or suggested the use of handbooks or handouts.

I had expected that reading aloud would be a factor in this study, but I was surprised at the pervasiveness of reading in the writing tutorials with deaf students. In my research I had learned that reading was difficult for them, but I had to see it myself before I realized the importance of reading to the way deaf students learn. Kali read a good deal and enjoyed it, Blue wanted to read more but found it difficult, and Rae found that her understanding of her textbook varied with the qualities of the writing; she admitted that she was unlikely to read long printouts of information from the Internet.

The tutoring focus of reading comprehension is one of the main differences between the deaf and the hearing tutees in this study. Vocabulary was also an issue. Blue commented, "I'm so sick of those big words I don't understand," and her tutor, Newby, pointed out, "If you don't know the vocabulary, and you look the word up, and you don't know the words that are used to define it, and you don't have a good grip on written language . . . you are in a double bind." At times I also noticed that the sentences that perplexed tutors, the ones they had to read over and over, were instances of paraphrase. It is difficult to paraphrase something that you do not understand.

Efficacy of Common Tutoring Techniques

Many of the same tutoring techniques are used with equal effectiveness with both deaf and hearing tutees, including asking real questions for information, giving suggestions and advice, and discussing ideas. In this section I highlight only those practices that pose different issues when used with deaf students: reading aloud and directiveness. I also discuss monitoring and issues of authority, especially tutors' advocating for teacher authority during the tutorial.

Reading Aloud

I had expected reading aloud to be a factor in the study, and it was. Actually, I did not know what to expect when it came to reading aloud in the tutoring session. Marron (1993) read aloud in a tutorial with a deaf student (and no interpreter) until she realized what she was doing, felt silly, and stopped. Obviously, if there is no interpreter, reading aloud to a deaf student, who would have to read the tutor's lips or receive an incomplete auditory input, is much less efficient than reading along together on paper. Traditionally, the goal of reading aloud is for the students to hear their own errors. In reference to ESL students, Powers writes, "These techniques, which largely involve reading aloud and using the ear to edit, presume that the writer hears the language correctly and is more familiar and comfortable with the oral than the written word" (2001, 371). This could apply to deaf tutees as well.

Reading aloud was sometimes done for the tutor's benefit. At certain points in the study I heard tutors reading aloud in a low, almost mumbling tone. This was not meant to be interpreted; rather, it was so the tutor could understand the paper. The interpreter would sometimes transliterate what was written, sometimes sign "She's reading," and sometimes direct the tutee's attention to the paper so the tutee could read along. Deaf people can perceive English on paper, on the hands, and on the lips. The choice of whether to read aloud and have it transliterated or to read together on the paper is one that must be negotiated among tutor, tutee, and interpreter. Sometimes the participants will have different goals for the reading. At one point in the tutoring sessions I observed, Newby said to Blue, "I'm gonna read [aloud]. You tell me how it sounds." Immediately Linda stopped her and asked, "What do you mean?" Later, in an interview, Linda said that she really did not know what the tutor meant:

> Linda: I think what happens is that tutors forget that deaf people
>   have never heard English, and they don't know what it

sounds like. And I don't think that they mean, "Does that—
is that a—is that sentence grammatically correct?" I think
they mean, "Does that sound correct?" I don't think that
they're meaning metaphorically. I think they literally mean
"What does that sound like?" . . .

Rebecca: That's the way they perceive English.

Linda: That's the way they perceive English.

Rebecca: Through the ear.

Linda: Any hearing person who's never . . . had . . . even just a
           moment to really . . . think about this—they're not gonna get
           that. And it's just . . . ignorance. It's just that they don't know.

Rebecca: That's the way we talk, so we don't reflect . . .

Linda: On what our words really mean.

This brief conversation illustrates how important it is for tutors of deaf
students to carefully consider their choices of words. I had originally
called this book *Tell Me How It Sounds* to stress this phenomenon, but
there was a danger that readers would not see the irony.

Reading aloud in tutoring sessions goes beyond just the tutor reading
to the tutee. Interestingly, the disabilities services coordinator at Stanhope
told me it can be helpful for deaf students to sign what they have written. Storm (1987), who worked with deaf students at the Clarke School
(an oral deaf school), actually recommends that deaf students read their
work aloud. At times I observed tutees signing what they wrote in the
tutoring sessions.

Directiveness

I had anticipated that the issue of directiveness would be relevant to the
study both because Deaf culture values it and because the efficacy of nondirective tutoring has been criticized for use with ESL students and students with learning disabilities (Blau, Hall, and Sparks 2002; Scanlon 1985).
Deaf students and their different learning styles and needs mirror those of
the latter students to some extent. Blau, Hall and Sparks (2002) show that
questioning techniques with ESL students frequently turn into closed and
directed questions in a game of "Guess what tutor knows." This is what

happened with Newby and Blue in the "youngest of nine children" (48) and "wanted her for a job" (81) sequences, both of which involved a particular preposition that the tutor knew but wanted the tutee to guess at. However, when the session focuses on grammar and correctness, the tutor should take more control (Blau, Hall, and Sparks 2002). It is a waste of time to use Socratic questioning to attempt to elicit a construction that the student does not know. All of the tutors used both directive and nondirective techniques at times with deaf students and students with learning disabilities, and both approaches were effective at times. However, nondirective techniques often proved frustrating, and directive techniques, although discouraged in training, appeared to be both effective and appropriate.

Monitoring and Authority

I was surprised to see the tutors frequently advocating for the teachers' authority and upholding their expectations. I had expected to see the tutee be the one who suggested they follow the assignment or make sure the teacher's requirements were being met, but it was almost always the tutor who did so. This is perhaps because two of the three tutors in the study are professional (MA degreed), not peer, tutors. It could also be a result of tutor training, as tutors are encouraged to make sure the student is following the assignment. It may also result from a sense of responsibility; as John and Gustav mentioned, they are responsible for seeing that their tutees meet the teachers' expectations. In only one instance did the tutor and the tutee deliberately subvert the teacher's authority, and this was in a tutorial with the only peer tutor in the study.

Contributing and Complicating Factors

I had anticipated that communication would be a complicating factor in the tutoring sessions since deaf people and hearing people communicate differently. Also, my objective was to study the feelings surrounding the tutoring sessions since many studies ignore this important facet of learning. Other pertinent factors were cultural factors and the participants' learning styles.

Communication

Communication was one of my original research interests. I wanted to know how communication occurred and whether one method was preferable. This conclusion was easy. As I learned more about deaf people and Deaf culture, I realized the preferred communication model is whatever the deaf person favors. Although tutorials between a deaf student and a hearing tutor can take place with a variety of communication models, in this study all of the relevant tutoring sessions took place with a sign language interpreter. The participants said that the main difference between a tutoring session with a hearing student and one with a deaf student was the presence of an interpreter. In all of the tutoring sessions I observed, communication was facilitated by an interpreter. So, the primary difference between tutoring a deaf student and tutoring a hearing student is communication (Hodge and Preston-Sabin 1997).

Most of the participants said that communication was not a problem and that the interpreters were doing a good job. Kali mentioned that she did not have a good experience with all of her tutors and that she did not like it when the interpreters used ASL. The interpreters who participated in the study told me, however, that they gear their language use to the desire of the deaf student. For instance, Kali prefers more English-like signing, so interpreter Melissa uses signs in English word order. The interpreter should be skilled enough to be able to match the language of the deaf student's preference. Some interpreters are certified by the Registry for Interpreters for the Deaf as transliterators (spoken English to signed English), and some are registered as interpreters (English/ASL). An interpreter may be nationally certified in only one of these areas or certified only by the state. Melissa told me that most educational interpreting is transliterating word for word into English.

Also, when discussing text in the tutoring session, sometimes it is more helpful just to have the deaf student read what is on the page instead of the interpreter transliterating what the tutor may read aloud. Linda, another interpreter, said, "When you're interpreting something that's related to English, it makes sense to actually have people read in English because once it gets interpreted into sign, it's back to square one again." However, Jay, who interpreted for Blue, said sometimes Blue would prefer the tutor to read aloud and have the interpreter sign the information.

Jay explained that it is almost impossible to sign English words exactly, but one can mouth them while signing a close approximation. At one point in their tutoring sessions, Newby asked Jay not to interpret because she preferred that Blue read the text herself. Linda recommended that the more conversational part of the tutoring session be done in ASL and the part precisely about English be done in a signed modality of English. Jay also talked about using English signing when the content was explicitly about the English language. Of course, this is according to the tutee's preference.

Linda also talked about the issues of voice and word choice. Writing tutoring often focuses on word choice, a topic that came up more than once in this study. When a deaf tutee signs in ASL, the interpreter chooses an appropriate English word as an equivalent. This is sometimes difficult, as Linda explains:

> The problem comes in when a deaf person brainstorms in ASL. . . . I make an interpretation. . . . I would use my word choice. Really, I'm using words that they would use in their language that match their educational background, economical, socio, you know, what-ever, but that's not always the case. So, sometimes what happens . . . [is that] the tutor will say, "Oh, I like that word you used." But that's the interpreter's word.

Interestingly enough, almost everyone I talked to in the study said it would be a good idea to have tutors who knew sign language to tutor deaf students. Since they are doing this at Gallaudet University and Harper College, it might be taken as a model—after investigation, of course. The tutor's sign language skill is very important. In a college classroom, students would much rather work with an interpreter or a captioning system than with a teacher with weak signing skills (Schmitz 2008). Thus, it is very important that a beginner who has had only one or two classes in sign language should not tutor a deaf student without an interpreter.

Feelings

The participants felt mostly positive about the sessions. Some of the tutees criticized former tutors or interpreters, and perhaps the nature of the research prevented any of them from saying anything negative about their current tutors or interpreters. Both tutors and tutees felt grateful for the tutoring experience. Some, like Squirt, felt frustrated, whereas most felt happy and comfortable in the tutoring session. Squirt, although vexed, also said she experienced happiness and joy during the tutoring sessions. The tutees also felt more confident because of the tutoring sessions. However, as mentioned earlier, one tutee was uncomfortable with the observations and declined further participation.

Learner's Characteristics

Most people have three learning channels—kinesthetic, auditory, and visual—available to them (Hodge and Preston-Sabin 1997; Konstant 1992; Ryan 1998). Students who are profoundly deaf rely on the visual channel and, for obvious reasons, are visual learners. Understanding different modalities of processing language will benefit not only those students who cannot use one or more of the learning channels but also those whose preferences or abilities favor learning that is not focused on oral/aural production and processing of language.

I noticed two main preferred learning styles in the deaf students I worked with. Rae and Blue favored watching the interpreter, and Kali was partial to learning by reading. Blue expressed the desire to read more, improve her vocabulary, and understand what she read. Rae preferred to read books with pictures or text that evoked a visual image. Tutors used visual means of communicating with deaf students, such as putting a text in view of both tutor and tutee and reading it together.

Sometimes the deaf tutees in this study seemed quite passive, as they frequently gave one-word answers to the tutors' questions and explanations. This could be a factor of the students themselves or of the tutors. A few times Rae took the reins and drove the session, as did Kali, but Blue did so only minimally. This may illustrate the nature of Rae and Kali as learners. Deaf students expressed appreciation for directiveness, as did Squirt, the study's one hearing student with a learning disability. (Deaf student Rae also has a learning disability.) Although it would be easy to say all students want the tutor to simply correct their papers, Harris (1995, 30–31) has found that students were more satisfied with tutorials in which the tutor asked them to think through their own writing than with those in which the tutor controlled the situation. The key differences between deaf-hearing and hearing-hearing tutorials seem to be the appropriateness of the directiveness factor and whether hearing and having an "ear" for the language are stressed. In tutorials with deaf students, rules of grammar appear to be emphasized rather than what "sounds right."

Culture

I had expected culture to factor more significantly in this study than it actually did. Although culture influenced the actual tutoring sessions only minimally, it affected me more as a researcher when cultural expectations clashed with my research techniques. The data-gathering techniques used in qualitative research methods are culturally specific, it seems, to mainstream American hearing culture. As I attempted to use semistructured, qualitative interview techniques, I realized they were not working as I wished.

I was wondering why I could not get Blue to open up to me in the interviews. Of course, I blamed her, thinking she was shy or reticent, that she was not outgoing, or even that she did not trust me. I brought my concern to interpreter Jay, as interpreters do more than interpret words; they also interpret cultures. Jay told me that by using the qualitative interview techniques I had learned, I was being culturally insensitive. I had learned that researchers should ask general, open-ended questions to get the participant to talk and not put the answer they want to get in the question (Rubin and Rubin 1995). Jay told me that in Deaf culture this method is all wrong. Even though I had been reading about and studying Deaf culture, I was amused and embarrassed as a researcher to learn that my cultural insensitivity had caused some misunderstanding. Jay explained it to me in an interview:

Rebecca: I want maybe some advice on how to open Blue up. I feel she's not opening up to me. And I don't know if it's the way I'm asking questions, or she doesn't . . . trust . . . me, or any advice on how I can get her to lay it all out—just tell me everything. [laughs] Or is that just how she is?

Jay: Deaf culture and hearing culture are different. . . .

Rebecca: I've been reading about it. I've been trying to learn.

Jay: Exactly. So you know the culture's totally different. I don't
              think she's being introverted or not trying to give out too
              much, but I think the questions you might ask are a little,
              you know, fluffy, not straightforward questions. That's what
              I'm trying to say. A little vague. You're thinking, "She'll
              get the hint if I just say this . . .," but you need to . . . be
              straightforward and just ask what you want to know. . . . I
              have a Deaf aunt, so I have some experience in that area.
              I have a Deaf aunt and uncle, actually. And I know for a
              fact, if they really want . . . to know something, they're just
              gonna come out and say it. They're not gonna use the little
              nice words—

Rebecca: I feel so silly. Because I should know all that because I have
              read about that and been told that before, and I guess I'm
              thinking if I just ask a general question, she'll just start tell-
              ing me everything.

Jay: That's hearing culture. . . .

Rebecca: But a couple things I asked . . . "What about this folder?"
              And she told me. And . . . "What works for you in tutoring?
              What do you want to learn?" She did tell me she wanted to
              learn more vocabulary. So . . . what I'm afraid of, in all my
              books on how to interview, you're not supposed to give too
              much information in the question. . . . You have to be very
              vague and let the person give you the information, but that's
              not gonna work.

Jay: Different culture. . . . Find a way to phrase your questions
              differently. Because you don't want to offend, and you want
              to be aware of Deaf cultural needs and [have] more sensitiv-
              ity. But in the Deaf culture, it's just a different culture. You
              have to approach it that way.

Rebecca: And I'm afraid, like from my interviewing books and stuff,
              that if you put—you don't want to put the answer in the
              question. You don't want to be too specific about what
              information you're looking for because then that's like, I
              don't know, in our hearing culture.

Jay: . . . That's exactly what she is looking for. I mean, when you ask her a question . . . I've noticed sometimes with the questions she's like, "What do you mean?" or "You mean this?" . . .

Rebecca: "Tell me about the tutoring session." "Tell you what?"

Jay: "Tell you what?" Right. So, you have to . . . say, "I wanna know this, and I wanna know this, and I wanna know this, and if you don't want to answer this, fine, but I wanna know this." So, I think that'll help if you're really clear and really straightforward.

Rebecca: [looking through notebook] Let me tell you what I'm gonna ask her, and you tell me if I'm—I tried to be more specific. I'm gonna ask her, "How do you learn best?" Is that straightforward enough?

Jay: But then she's gonna say, "What do you mean, learn best?"

Rebecca: What is your learning style? Do you learn by reading? By doing?

Jay: That's getting to the meat of it.

Rebecca: OK.

Jay: . . . More specific. . . . You may want to put the answers in the questions. If that's the answer, or if you want a straight yes or no, or if you want an answer from that, then . . .

Rebecca: OK.

Jay: You have to try.

I offer this long excerpt because it might help other hearing researchers who are working with Deaf people. If you want to know about something, be explicit in your questions.

Newby also mentioned the need to be clear rather than vague when asking a Deaf person a question. This example can also help researchers working with other cultures to be sensitive to their norms. Like a tutor changing techniques when working with different tutees, researchers, too, must be sensitive to the cultures of the people they are working with and abandon methods such as open-ended interview questions, which may be seen as inappropriate in the target culture.

The few cultural issues that did occur in the tutorial were related to sensitivity to the Deaf experience, like being aware of what it means

to not be able to hear. This became clear in some of the exchanges
between Blue and Newby. I originally thought time would turn out to
be a major cultural issue. As it turned out, it was not, although some of
the participants mentioned that it would be a good thing to have more
time to tutor a deaf student. The one tutorial I observed that took place
by writing on paper took well over an hour.

Recommendations for Practice

Most important, I recommend that writing centers open their doors
to everyone. With the coming of students who are different, whether
physically or in the way they learn, writing center practitioners have to
be ready to help anyone who comes in that open door. What follows are
some recommendations that grew out of this study relating to the preparation of tutors to work with deaf students in particular. Interestingly, two
of the tutors in the study said that one cannot actually be trained to tutor;
rather, it is a skill one must learn by doing.

Tutor Training

I recommend that every tutor who works in a writing center in an
institution with a deaf population learn, at a minimum, the manual
alphabet. The reason for this is that fingerspelling is the only way to
precisely represent written English on the hands. Ideally all of the
tutors—and by extension all college faculty and staff and even hearing
people in general—should learn a little sign language and be familiar
with the properties and varieties of signed languages and the basics of
Deaf culture. Daisy, the disabilities services director at Stanhope, also
recommends this.

I suggest that writing center directors, if they control who tutors
whom, take into consideration the qualities of understanding, patience,
and potential rapport when pairing tutors with deaf students. Familiarity
with ESL methods, special education, learning disabilities, and different learning styles would also be a plus, but as Rae's case illustrates, just
because a tutor has a graduate degree or is a professional or even an

instructor at the college does not necessarily mean that person will be a better tutor for a deaf person than an undergraduate.

Training in working with deaf students and, by extension, all students with sensory and physical disabilities, should be discussed in all tutor-training books and included in every program. This material could include instruction on how to work effectively with an interpreter, a brief overview of Deaf culture, and information on when and how standard tutoring methods do not work and how to modify or discard them and choose different ones when working with deaf people or others who learn differently.

Daisy recommends that tutors be familiar with readings on dialect and language interference in writing. Although my research has caused me to be skeptical of the importance of dialect/language interference, I agree that readings on the subject will be useful in tutor training, and all sides should be represented. If there is any influence of this type, it may be from glossing, which is the use of English words to represent signs, a practice that is employed because there is no standard, convenient, or widely accepted writing system for ASL. Deaf people often use glossing in text messages and email, as do some students who are working on experimental writing projects for classes (Harmon 2003). However, in these cases the language being used is ASL even though it is being written with English words (glosses). One solution to this problem would be to implement a common, accepted writing system for ASL.[8]

Another possible reason for ASL's apparent influence on deaf students' writing is the theory that Deaf students who use contact signing in English word order believe they are signing correct English (Mashie 1995). When they transcribe their signs word for word, the resulting text lacks features like articles that are dropped in contact signing. A solution to this problem would be to give deaf students a strong foundation in ASL and to reserve English for reading and writing only (Kuntze 2004).

---

8. The interdependence hypothesis says that to be bilingual one must have a firm foundation in the native language, so writing ASL is crucial for those whose native language is ASL. A very small number of people have ASL as a native language, however.

Practical Techniques

Here I discuss some specific techniques that worked well in the tutoring sessions I observed and some that were not so effective. I address the practitioner directly (i.e., in the second person).

Most of all, try to find out what the deaf person needs and wants out of the session, and gear your tutoring toward that. This will be uncomfortable, for instance, if the tutee asks for help with editing and proofreading and the tutor's training forbids that kind of assistance. Remember that deaf people cannot hear the nuances of English in order correct their errors by "hearing" their mistakes the way hearing students do. They must find their errors by sight, and many deaf college students are not as familiar with print as one would expect a college freshman to be.

Be patient and understanding as you find ways to help students find and correct their own errors. Reading aloud, which is a common tutoring technique, can pose problems for deaf students, who by definition cannot hear. Thus, the traditional objective for reading aloud, that of hearing one's mistakes, does not apply. For deaf students and students like Shareef who speak a nonstandard dialect, reading aloud as the only technique to catch errors will not work. These students need to learn to see the errors on the page, and in order to do this they must be familiar with the conventions of print in English, and that is best done by reading.

In addition, you need to pay special attention to reading comprehension, paraphrasing, and summarizing with a deaf tutee, much more so than you would with a hearing tutee. To this end, the tutor has to be a cheerleader for reading. Find out whether your deaf tutee reads a lot. If the answer is "Yes," you should notice a more standard product. If the answer is "No," then encourage your tutee to read. You could do like Newby did and recommend books, go to the library together, or even give your tutees a book that you think they might enjoy. I gave the deaf participants in the study gift certificates to Barnes and Noble. During the member-checking phase of this study I was encouraged when Blue said she could not respond to the chapters as she was reading a book and did not want to divide her attention between the book and the chapters at the same time. Composition scholars Tonya Stremlau and

Brenda Brueggemann (who are deaf and hard of hearing, respectively) both attribute their success with English to voracious reading early on. Study participants Newby and Kali feel the same way, as do I. The key to the entire puzzle seems to be reading. Start reading early and keep reading and you will be all right. Marlon Kuntze (pers. comm.) says reading, along with a strong foundation in ASL, is the key to d/Deaf students' literacy success.

Make sure you give the deaf person opportunity for more than one-word answers. To check understanding, you could ask the student to rephrase what you have been talking about. In addition, although it is uncomfortable to leave silences, wait and give the deaf person a chance to enter the conversation rather than talk on and on. Remember, what hearing people think of as open-ended questions, deaf people may find vague. Try asking direct, pointed *wh*-questions rather than ones that require only a yes-or-no answer. You could use imperatives, which lead to talk more so than questions (Johnson 1993).

Although nondirective techniques are valued in many writing centers, these methods may not work very well with deaf writers. I have also learned from observation and research that these approaches may not be very effective with ESL students and students with learning disabilities, either. However, all writers still need to be pushed to find their own answers whenever possible. Deaf students may be frustrated by nondirective questioning, especially in light of their culture's value of directness. I recommend that, with deaf students and students with learning disabilities, tutors try nondirective techniques but abandon them if they prove unproductive (Neff 1994; Blau, Hall, and Sparks 2002; Shamoon and Burns 1995). Be direct with deaf people, too, as their culture values it.

Blue valued Newby's practice of sitting next to her and holding the paper so both of them could see it. An important technique when working with a deaf student is sharing texts. Other uses of written text are those Rae and John employed: Rae typed her answers directly into the computer so John could read them on screen and comment as she typed. Also, John took notes for Rae as she signed her answers. Both of these techniques are promising ways to share language, text, and ideas.

When discussing text, be careful not to split the tutee's attention between the text and the interpreter. A deaf person cannot attend to the text *and* the interpreter at the same time, although a hearing person can sometimes read and listen at the same time. If you want to tell a deaf student something while the student is looking down at the text, you will have to stop the student (do this by waving your hand in the student's field of vision) and wait until the student's attention is focused on the interpreter, then give your message. Likewise, if you are talking and want the deaf person to attend to something on the paper, finish talking, let the interpreter finish interpreting, then focus the deaf student's attention on the paper. This is hard to understand for hearing people, who can take in an aural and a visual message at the same time, but a deaf person can take in only one visual message at a time, either the interpreter's signs or the words on the paper.

When working with deaf students on grammar and mechanical conventions, it is important for tutors to be sensitive to the tutees' needs. A tutee might want a verbal explanation, a handout, a trip to the grammar book, or just a fixed error. I recommend the tutor ask the tutee what kind of help is needed, and if a detailed explanation would be welcomed, give it in the format the tutee prefers. Deaf participant Rae values her tutor's giving advice and explanations but not ones that are too technical in reference to grammatical rules. The explanations can be given in technical or nontechnical terms, depending on the student's interest in grammar as a topic of study. Also, modeling a correction can be effective for a visual learner, with or without an explanation. This is especially true for difficult rules of grammar that the tutor might not even know, such as the rules of article use in English. When Kali asked Gustav about article use during a tutorial, he modeled the correction and told her the rule was too complicated and that he did not know it himself. This kind of honesty is superior to giving a half-learned or half-correct version of a rule.

When working with an interpreter, make sure you address the deaf person and not the interpreter. Also, consult the deaf person about the ideal seating arrangements. Check with the deaf person and the interpreter, too, about the most efficient way to communicate written information. Sometimes the best idea is to direct the deaf person's attention to the written text, sometimes the tutor can read it aloud and the interpreter interpret, and sometimes the deaf person can sign what is written on the page. Linda, one of the interpreters in the study, said, "When you're interpreting something that's related to English, it makes sense to actually have people read in English." These techniques can be used for the student's own writing, as well as for other texts. Which one is appropriate should be negotiated by the tutor, the tutee, and the interpreter.

When producing text, the student can write for the tutor directly on paper or the computer screen or sign while the interpreter interprets and the tutor takes notes. Again, the format and technique should be negotiated among the participants. Sometimes the tutor will have a genuine educational reason for preferring one method or the other, or the interpreter or student will have a communicative or linguistic preference. For instance, interpreter Linda reflected that it is easier for a deaf person to brainstorm in ASL as the ideas can come freely without the need to translate them into English. In another example, John asked the interpreter, "Should I read this out loud, and then you just relay it to her, or—?" and Rae responded, "I'll read it myself." This is a good model of how to negotiate the communication method and the transfer of information.

Do not waste the tutee's time with your own questions and curiosities. The tutoring time belongs to the tutee, not to you. You as a tutor are being paid to help the student, not for the student to educate you about deafness. If you are interested in the topic—and you should be if you are tutoring a deaf student—you can get a book on the subject such as *Inside Deaf Culture* (Padden and Humphries 2006), *A Journey into the* DEAF-WORLD (Lane, Hoffmeister, and Bahan 1996), *Reading between the Signs* (Mindess 1999), *American Deaf Culture* (Wilcox 1989), or *Through Deaf Eyes* (Baynton, Gannon, and Bergey 2007). You could also talk to your school's disabilities services coordinator for suggestions.

Moreover, some schools offer courses in Deaf culture and ASL. If you are particularly interested in talking to the tutee personally about these issues, ask to meet outside the tutoring session at a mutually convenient time and place so as not to monopolize the tutee's tutoring time. Perhaps you could tell the tutee of your interest, and the tutee could answer your questions on a day when he or she does not have an assignment to work on in the tutoring session. If you are interested in Deaf culture and deaf people, another idea is to volunteer to be an in-class notetaker for a deaf student.

Conclusions

The simple answer to what happens in a tutoring session is that people learn to write; in other words, they learn the literacy practices of an unfamiliar discourse community, in this case, the academic discourse community. More specifically for this study, the participants were eager to learn the use of standard American English, with its conventions and related skills, as well as the receptive ability to understand reading and vocabulary. The exception to this is Herrodrick, the only hearing white suburban male in the study, who spent most of his tutoring sessions talking about the ideas he was writing about. His focus could have something to do with his majority status. All of the other study participants, whether hearing or deaf, were either minorities or women, and perhaps this otherness added to their desire to acquire new discourses.

Reading was brought up in almost all of the tutoring sessions with deaf people I observed. Perhaps this is because it is the only fully accessible, direct avenue to English for deaf people (Johnson 1996; Kuntze 2004). In all, tutoring sessions involving a deaf tutee and a hearing tutor are very similar to sessions between two hearing people. With a few exceptions, the actual tutoring practices are quite the same for both hearing and deaf students. Almost all of the sessions I observed contained elements of directiveness, nondirectiveness, and collaboration.

Although the tutoring practices that a hearing tutor employs with a hearing student on the one hand and a deaf student on the other can be very similar, common tutoring practices of reading aloud and nondirectiveness can be problematic for deaf students and others who learn differently, such as students with learning disabilities. I also discovered that in tutorials on writing, reading is a major factor. Students' reading behavior and background appear to directly affect their writing performance, their attitude, and their school performance overall. Deaf students, like other students, are all different and cannot be expected to all learn in the same way. In general, all students are unique, and work with deaf students not only reinforces that fact but also demonstrates in a very real and practical way how different tutoring practices must be adapted and adopted for a variety of students and populations.

Bibliography

American Psychological Association. 2001. *Publication Manual of the American Psychological Association,* 5th ed. Washington, DC: Author.

Ameter, B., and C. Dahl. 1990. Coordination and Cooperation: A Writing Center Serves a Hearing Impaired Student. *Writing Lab Newsletter* 14 (February): 4–5.

Arkin, M., and B. Shollar. 1982. *The Tutor Book.* New York: Longman.

Babcock, R. D. 2006. The Influence of ASL on Deaf Students' Written English Texts. Paper presented at the 122nd annual meeting of the Modern Language Association, Philadelphia, December 27–30.

———. 2008. Tutoring Deaf College Students in Writing. In *Disability and the Teaching of Writing: A Critical Sourcebook,* ed. B. J. Brueggemann and C. Lewiecki-Wilson, 28–39. New York: Bedford–St. Martin's.

———. 2009. Research-Based Tutoring Tips for Working with Deaf Students. *Kansas English* 93 (1): 73–98.

———. 2011. Interpreted Writing Center Tutorials with College-Level Deaf Students. *Linguistics and Education* 22 (2): 95–117.

Ballenger, C. 1992. Because You Like Us: The Language of Control. *Harvard Educational Review* 62 (Summer): 199–208.

Barnes, L. 2006. Formal Qualifications for Language Tutors in Higher Education: A Case for Discussion. *Deafness and Education International* 8 (3): 106–24.

Barnett, R., and J. Blumner, eds. 2001. *The Allyn and Bacon Guide to Writing Center Theory and Practice.* Boston: Allyn and Bacon.

Baynton, D., J. R. Gannon, and J. Bergey. 2007. *Through Deaf Eyes: A Photographic History of an American Community.* Washington, DC: Gallaudet University Press.

Blau, S. R., J. Hall, J. Davis, and L. Gravitz. 2001. Tutoring ESL Students: A Different Kind of Session. *Writing Lab Newsletter* 25 (June): 1–4.

Blau, S. R., J. Hall, and S. Sparks. 2002. Guilt-Free Tutoring: Rethinking How We Tutor Non-Native-English-Speaking Students. *Writing Center Journal* 23: 23–44.

Brooks, J. 1991. Minimalist Tutoring: Making the Student Do All the Work. *Writing Lab Newsletter* 15 (February): 1–4.

Brueggemann, B. J. 1992. Context and Cognition in the Composing Processes of Two Deaf Writers. PhD diss., University of Louisville. Abstract. *Dissertation Abstracts International* 54 (01A): 0159.

Campbell, D. R. 1986. Developing Mathematical Literacy in a Bilingual Classroom. In *The Social Construction of Literacy*, ed. J. Cook-Gumperz, 156–84. New York: Cambridge University Press.

Capposella, T.-L. 1998. *Harcourt Brace Guide to Peer Tutoring*. New York: Harcourt Brace.

Carino, P. 1995. Early Writing Centers: Toward a History. *Writing Center Journal* 15: 103–15. Reprinted in *The Allyn and Bacon Guide to Writing Center Theory and Practice*, ed. R. Barnett and J. Blumner, 10–21. Boston: Allyn and Bacon, 2001.

————. 2003. Power and Authority in Peer Tutoring. In *The Center Will Hold*, ed. M. A. Pemberton and J. Kinkead, 96–113. Logan: Utah State University Press.

Chappell, V. A. 1982. Hands Off: Fostering Self-Reliance in the Writing Lab. *Writing Lab Newsletter* 6 (February): 4–6.

Charmaz, K. 2000. Grounded Theory: Objectivist and Constructivist Methods. In *Handbook of Qualitative Research*, ed. N. K. Denzin and Y. S. Lincoln, 509–35. Thousand Oaks, CA: Sage.

Clark, B. L. 1985. *Talking about Writing*. Ann Arbor: University of Michigan Press.

Clark, I. L., and D. Healy. 1996. Are Writing Centers Ethical? *Writing Program Administration* 20: 32–48.

Condron, D. J., and V. J. Roscigno. 2003. Disparities Within: Unequal Spending and Achievement in an Urban School District. *Sociology of Education* 76 (1): 18–36.

Davis, C. D., and M. R. Smith. 2000. Effective Tutoring Practices with Deaf and Hard of Hearing Students. *2000 PEPNet Conference Proceedings*, ed. K. B. Jursik, 102–8. http://www.pepnet.org/resources/2000conf.

Davis, L. J. 1995. The Deafened Moment as a Critical Modality. *College English* 57: 881–900.

Day, R. 2002. "Tutoring Deaf and Hard of Hearing Students." Paper presented at the National Conference on Peer Tutoring in Writing, Midwest Writing Centers Association, Lawrence, KS, October 26.

Delpit, L. 1988. The Silenced Dialogue: Power and Pedagogy in Educating Other People's Children. *Harvard Educational Review* 58 (August): 280–98.

Dulay, H., M. Burt, and S. Krashen. 1982. *Language Two.* New York: Oxford University Press.

Eckard, S. J., and J. E. Staben. 2000. Becoming a Resource: Multiple Ways of Thinking about Information and the Writing Conference. In *A Tutor's Guide,* ed. B. Rafoth, 135–46. Portsmouth, NH: Boynton/Cook.

Faerm, E. 1992. Tutoring Anne: A Case Study. *Writing Lab Newsletter* 16 (March): 9–10.

Fileccia, J. 2011. Sensitive Care for the Deaf: A Cultural Challenge. *Creative Nursing* 17 (4): n.p. Retrieved from Questia database.

Gannon, J. R. 1981. *Deaf Heritage: A Narrative History of Deaf America.* Silver Spring, MD: National Association of the Deaf.

Gillespie, P., and N. Lerner. 2000. *The Allyn and Bacon Guide to Peer Tutoring.* Boston: Allyn and Bacon.

———. 2003. *The Allyn and Bacon Guide to Peer Tutoring,* 2nd ed. Boston: Allyn and Bacon.

Greiner, A. 2000. Tutoring in Unfamiliar Subjects. In *A Tutor's Guide,* ed. B. Rafoth, 85–90. Portsmouth, NH: Heinemann.

Grimm, N. 1999. *Good Intentions.* Portsmouth, NH: Boynton/Cook.

Guralnik, D. B., gen. ed. 1964. *Concise Edition: Webster's New World Dictionary.* Cleveland: World Publishing.

Haas, T. S. 1986. A Case Study of Peer Tutors' Writing Conferences with Students: Tutors' Roles and Conversations about Composing. PhD diss., New York University, 1986. Abstract. *Dissertation Abstracts International* 47:4309.

Hacker, D. 2002. *A Writer's Reference,* 4th ed. Boston: Bedford.

Hall, S. 1989. Train-Gone-Sorry: The Etiquette of Conversations in American Sign Language. In *American Deaf Culture,* ed. S. Wilcox, 89–102. Burtonsville, MD: Linstok.

Harmon, K. 2003. "Textualizing Deaf Literature." Paper presented at the annual meeting of the Modern Language Association, San Diego, December 27–30.

Harris, M. 1986. *Teaching One-to-One: The Writing Conference.* Urbana, IL: NCTE.

———. 1995. Talking in the Middle: Why Writers Need Writing Tutors. *College English* 57: 27–42.

Hartwell, P. 1980. Dialect Interference in Writing: A Critical View. *Research in the Teaching of English* 14: 101–18.

Hayward, N. 2004. Insights into Cultural Divides. In *ESL Writers: A Guide for Writing Center Conferences,* ed. S. Bruce and B. Rafoth, 1–15. Portsmouth, NH: Boynton/Cook.

Heath, S. B. 1983. *Ways with Words.* Cambridge: Cambridge University Press.

Hodge, B. M., and J. Preston-Sabin, eds. 1997. *Accommodations—Or Just Good Teaching?* Westport, CT: Praeger.

Hubbuch, S. M. 1988. A Tutor Needs to Know the Subject Matter to Help a Student with a Paper: __Agree __Disagree __Not Sure. *Writing Center Journal* 8: 23–30.

Johnson, J. B. 1993. Reevaluation of the Question as a Teaching Tool. In *Dynamics of the Writing Conference,* ed. T. Flynn and M. King, 34–40. Urbana, IL: NCTE.

Johnson, T. S. 1996. Deaf Students in Mainstreamed College Composition Courses: Culture and Pedagogy. Abstract. *Dissertation Abstracts International* 57 (9): 3857A (UMI no. 9706338).

Kelly, L. P. 1987. The Influence of Syntactic Anomalies on the Writing of a Deaf College Student. In *Writing in Real Time: Modeling Production Processes,* ed. A. Matsuhashi, 161–96. Norwood, NJ: Ablex.

King, S. J., J. J. DeCaro, M. A. Karchmer, and K. J. Cole, eds. 2001. *College and Career Programs for Deaf Students,* 11th ed. http://research.gallaudet. edu/colleges.html (accessed August 29, 2012).

Kirsch, G. 1992. Methodological Pluralism: Epistemological Issues. In *Methods and Methodology in Composition Research,* ed. G. Kirsch and P. Sullivan, 247–69. Carbondale: Southern Illinois University Press.

———. 1999. *Ethical Dilemmas in Feminist Research.* Albany: State University of New York Press.

Konstant, S. 1992. Multisensory Tutoring for Multisensory Learners. *Writing Lab Newsletter* 16 (May–June): 6–8.

Krashen, S. 1982. *Principles and Practice in Second Language Acquisition.* New York: Prentice-Hall.

Kuntze, M. 2004. "Literacy and Signed Languages: Should Ever the Twain Meet?" Paper presented at the 120th meeting of the Modern Language Association, Philadelphia, December 27–30.

Kutz, E. 1997. *Language and Literacy.* Portsmouth, NH: Boynton/Cook.

Lane, H. 1992. *The Mask of Benevolence.* San Diego: DawnSignPress.

Lane, H., R. Hoffmeister, and B. Bahan. 1996. *A Journey into the* DEAF-WORLD. San Diego: DawnSignPress.

Lang, H. G. 2002. Higher Education for Deaf Students: Research Priorities in the New Millennium. *Journal of Deaf Studies and Deaf Education* 7: 267–80.

Lang, H. G., E. Biser, K. Mousley, R. Orlando, and J. Porter. 2004. Tutoring Deaf Students in Higher Education: A Comparison of Baccalaureate and Sub-baccalaureate Student Perceptions. *Journal of Deaf Studies and Deaf Education* 9: 189–201.

Lerner, N. 1996. Teaching and Learning in a University Writing Center. PhD diss., Boston University. Abstract. *Dissertation Abstracts International* 57:1060.

Lincoln, Y. S., and E. G. Guba. 1985. *Naturalistic Inquiry.* Newbury Park, CA: Sage.

———. 2000. Paradigmatic Controversies, Contradictions, and Emerging Confluences. In *Handbook of Qualitative Research,* ed. N. K. Denzin and Y. S. Lincoln, 163–88. Thousand Oaks, CA: Sage.

Lunsford, A. 1991. Collaboration, Control, and the Idea of a Writing Center. *Writing Center Journal* 12: 3–11. Reprinted in *The Allyn and Bacon Guide to Writing Center Theory and Practice,* ed. R. Barnett and J. Blumner, 92–99. Boston: Allyn and Bacon, 2001.

Marron, P. 1993. Tutoring a Deaf Student: Another View. *Writing Lab Newsletter* 17 (January): 15–16.

Mashie, S. N. 1995. *Educating Deaf Children Bilingually.* Washington, DC: Gallaudet University Pre-college Programs.

Maxwell, J. A. 1996. *Qualitative Research Design.* Thousand Oaks, CA: Sage.

Mayer, C. 2007. What Really Matters in the Early Literacy Development of Deaf Children. *Journal of Deaf Studies and Deaf Education* 12 (4): 411–31. doi:10.1093/deafed/enm020

McAndrew, D. A., and T. J. Reigstad. 2001. *Tutoring Writing: A Practical Guide for Conferences.* Portsmouth, NH: Heinemann.

Meyer, E., and L. Z. Smith. 1987. *The Practical Tutor.* New York: Oxford University Press.

Michaels, S. 1986. Narrative Presentations: An Oral Preparation for Literacy with First Graders. In *The Social Construction of Literacy,* ed. J. Cook-Gumperz, 110–37. Cambridge: Cambridge University Press.

Mindess, A. 1999. *Reading between the Signs.* Yarmouth, ME: Intercultural Press.

Murphy, C., and S. Sherwood. 2003. *The St. Martin's Sourcebook for Writing Tutors,* 2nd ed. New York: St. Martin's.

Nash, L. 2008. ESL in a Different Light: Can You Hear Me Now? *Writing Lab Newsletter* 32 (May): 1–5.

Neff, J. 1994. Learning Disabilities in the Writing Center. In *Intersections: Theory-Practice in the Writing Center,* ed. J. Mullin and R. Wallace. Reprinted in *The*

Allyn and Bacon Guide to Writing Center Theory and Practice, ed. R. Barnett and J. Blumner, 376–90. Boston: Allyn and Bacon, 2001.

North, S. 1984a. The Idea of a Writing Center. *College English* 46: 433–46. Reprinted in *The Allyn and Bacon Guide to Writing Center Theory and Practice,* ed. R. Barnett and J. Blumner, 63–78. Boston: Allyn and Bacon, 2001.

———. 1984b. Writing Center Research: Testing Our Assumptions. In *Writing Centers: Theory and Administration,* ed. G. A. Olson, 24–35. Urbana, IL: NCTE.

Olesen, V. L. 2000. Feminism and Qualitative Research at and into the Millennium. In *Handbook of Qualitative Research,* ed. N. K. Denzin and Y. S. Lincoln, 332–97. Thousand Oaks, CA: Sage.

Orlando, R., M. E. Gramly, and J. Hoke. 1997. *Tutoring Deaf and Hard of Hearing Students: A Report of the National Task Force on Quality of Services in the Postsecondary Education of Deaf and Hard of Hearing Students* (EC 307 622). Washington, DC: Office of Special Education and Rehabilitative Services. ERIC ED437774.

Osborne, H. 2003. Communicating about Health with ASL. *On Call* (June): 16–17.

Padden, C., and T. Humphries. 2006. *Inside Deaf Culture.* Cambridge, MA: Harvard University Press.

Paul, P. V. 1998. *Literacy and Deafness: The Development of Reading, Writing, and Literate Thought.* Boston: Allyn and Bacon.

Powers, J. 1993. Rethinking Writing Center Conferencing Strategies for the ESL Writer. *Writing Center Journal* 13: 39–47. Reprinted in *The Allyn and Bacon Guide to Writing Center Theory and Practice,* ed. R. Barnett and J. Blumner, 368–75. Boston: Allyn and Bacon, 2001.

Quigley, S. P., and Kretschmer, R. E. 1982. *The Education of Deaf Children.* Baltimore: University Park Press.

Quigley, S. P., and P. V. Paul. 1984. *Language and Deafness.* San Diego: College Hill Press.

Raue, K., & L. Lewis. 2011. *Students with Disabilities at Degree-Granting Postsecondary Institutions* (National Center for Education Statistics Report No. NCES 2011-018). Retrieved from http://nces.ed.gov/pubs2011/2011018.pdf.

Reigstad, T., and D. A. McAndrew. 1984. *Training Tutors for Writing Conferences.* Urbana, IL: NCTE.

Roy, C. 2000. *Interpreting as a Discourse Process.* New York: Oxford University Press.

Rubin, H. J., and I. S. Rubin. 1995. *Qualitative Interviewing.* Thousand Oaks, CA: Sage.

Ryan, L. 1998. *The Bedford Guide for Writing Tutors.* Boston: Bedford.

———. 2002. *The Bedford Guide for Writing Tutors,* 3d ed. Boston: Bedford.

Ryle, G. 1971. The Thinking of Thoughts: What Is "Le Penseur" Doing? In *Collected Essays: Collected Papers,* vol. 2. New York: Barnes and Noble.

Scanlon, L. C. 1985. Learning Disabled Students at the Writing Center. *Writing Lab Newsletter* 9 (January): 9–11.

Schmidt, K., M. Bunse, K. Dalton, N. Perry, and K. Rau. 2009. Lessening the Divide: Strategies for Promoting Effective Communication between Hearing Consultants and Deaf Student-Writers. *Writing Lab Newsletter* 33 (January): 6–10.

Schmitz, K. L. 2008. The Academic English Literacy Acquisition Experiences of Deaf College Students. PhD diss., State University of New York at Buffalo. https://ritdml.rit.edu/dspace/bit-stream/1850/6261/1/KSchmitzDissertation04-2008.pdf.

Schriver, K. A. 1992. Connecting Cognition and Context in Composition. In *Methods and Methodology in Composition Research,* ed. G. Kirsch and P. Sullivan, 190–216. Carbondale: Southern Illinois University Press.

Shamoon, L. K., and D. H. Burns. 1995. A Critique of Pure Tutoring. *Writing Center Journal* 15: 134–51. Reprinted in *The St. Martin's Sourcebook for Writing Tutors,* ed. C. Murphy and S. Sherwood, 173–88. Boston: Bedford/St. Martin's, 2003.

Stake, R. E. 1995. *The Art of Case Study Research.* Thousand Oaks, CA: Sage.

———. 2000. Case Studies. In *Handbook of Qualitative Research,* ed. N. K. Denzin and Y. S. Lincoln, 435–54. Thousand Oaks, CA: Sage.

Stinson, M. S., and E. R. Stuckless. 1998. Recent Developments in Speech-to-Print Transcription Systems for Deaf Students. In *Issues Unresolved,* ed. A. Weisel, 126–32. Washington, DC: Gallaudet University Press.

Stokoe, W. C., D. C. Casterline, and C. G. Croneberg. 1976. *A Dictionary of American Sign Language on Linguistic Principles.* Silver Spring, MD: Linstok. Originally published 1965.

Storm, R. D. 1987. Computer-Assisted Writing Program at Clarke School for the Deaf. In *Removing the Writing Barrier: A Dream? National Conference Proceedings: Innovative Writing Programs and Research for Deaf and Hearing Impaired Students.* Bronx: Lehman College, City University of New York.

Strauss, A., and J. Corbin. 1990. *Basics of Qualitative Research.* Newbury Park, CA: Sage.

————. 1998. *Basics of Qualitative Research,* 2nd ed. Thousand Oaks, CA: Sage.

Supalla, S. J. 1986. Manually Coded English: The Modality Question in Signed Language Development. Master's thesis, University of Illinois at Urbana-Champaign.

Swisher, M. V. 1989. The Language-Learning Situation of Deaf Students. *TESOL Quarterly* 23: 239–57.

Trimbur, J. 1987. Peer Tutoring: A Contradiction in Terms? *Writing Center Journal* 7: 21–28. Reprinted in *The Allyn and Bacon Guide to Writing Center Theory and Practice,* ed. R. Barnett and J. Blumner, 288–95. Boston: Allyn and Bacon, 2001.

Troyka, L. Q. 2001. *The Simon Schuster Handbook for Writers,* 6th ed. Upper Saddle River, NJ: Prentice Hall.

Tutor's Guide, The. 1986. Produced and directed by H. Naficy. Great Plains National. Videocassette.

Valli, C., and C. Lucas. 1992. *Linguistics of American Sign Language: A Resource Text for ASL Users.* Washington, DC: Gallaudet University Press.

Watson, D., J. G. Schroedel, M. Kolvitz, J. DeCaro, and D. Kavin, eds. 2007. *Hard of Hearing Students in Postsecondary Settings: A Guide for Service Providers.* Knoxville, TN: PEPNet-South.

Weaver, M. E. 1996. Transcending "Conversing": A Deaf Student in the Writing Center. *Journal of Advanced Composition* 16: 241–51. Retrieved from http://www.jaconlinejournal.com/archives/vol16.2/weaver-transcending.pdf.

Webster, A. 1986. *Deafness, Development, and Literacy.* New York: Methuen.

Wilcox, S., ed. 1989. *American Deaf Culture.* Bartonsville, MD: Linstok.

Wood, G. F. 1995. Making the Transition from ASL to English: Deaf Students, Computers, and the Writing Center. *Computers and Composition* 12: 219–26.

Index